Communication
Principles for a Lifetime
Portable Edition

Volume 2: Interpersonal Communication

STEVEN A. BEEBE
Texas State University–San Marcos

SUSAN J. BEEBE
Texas State University–San Marcos

DIANA K. IVY
Texas A&M University–Corpus Christi

Boston   New York   San Francisco
Mexico City   Montreal   Toronto   London   Madrid   Munich   Paris
Hong Kong   Singapore   Tokyo   Cape Town   Sydney

Editor in Chief: *Karon Bowers*
Series Editorial Assistant: *Jessica Cabana*
Marketing Manager: *Suzan Czajkowski*
Production Supervisor: *Beth Houston*
Editorial Production Service: *Lifland et al., Bookmakers*
Composition Buyer: *Linda Cox*
Manufacturing Buyer: *JoAnne Sweeney*
Electronic Composition: *Publishers' Design and Production Services, Inc.*
Photo Researcher: *Helane Prottas*
Cover Administrator: *Joel Gendron*

For related titles and support materials, visit our online catalog at www.ablongman.com.

Between the time website information is gathered and then published, it is not unusual for some sites to have closed. Also, the transcription of URLs can result in typographical errors. The publisher would appreciate notification where these errors occur so that they may be corrected in subsequent editions.

Library of Congress Cataloging-in-Publication Data

Beebe, Steven A., 1950–
    Communication: principles for a lifetime/Steven A. Beebe, Susan J. Beebe,
Diana K. Ivy—Portable ed.
        v. cm.
    Includes bibliographical references and index.
    ISBN-13: 978-0-205-59356-9
    1. Communication. I. Beebe, Susan J. II. Ivy, Diana K. III. Beebe, Susan J.
IV. Ivy, Diana K. V. Title.
    HM1206.B44 2009
    302.2—dc22   2007051355

ISBN-13: 978-0-205-59356-9   ISBN-10: 0-205-59356-9

Printed in the United States of America

10 9 8 7 6 5 4 3 2 1   RRD-IN   11 10 09 08

Contents

Preface

This portable edition of *Communication: Principles for a Lifetime* is for students on the move—those who, on a daily basis, commute, travel, or work and therefore must study in nontraditional settings. The portable edition contains four separate volumes, enabling students to take with them wherever they go, for both reading and self-assessment purposes, only the volume they need.

Students may take only one course in communication during their entire college career. Yet they need to remember essential communication principles and skills for the rest of their lives. In this portable edition of *Communication: Principles for a Lifetime*, our goal is to provide a cogent presentation of what is fundamental to human communication by applying to the study of communication five principles that are inherent in the process of communicating with others.

Communication is essential for life. We want students to view this course not simply as another course in a string of curricular requirements or options, but as a vital, life-enriching course that will help them enhance their communication with others.

The Challenge of a Fundamentals of Communication Course

Most introductory communication courses cover a vast terrain of communication concepts, principles, and skills. Besides several theories of communication, students are presented with what may appear to them to be abbreviated courses in interpersonal communication, group communication, and public speaking. In addition to developing a conceptual understanding of communication, students are expected to master communication skills, including group discussion and problem-solving skills, listening and paraphrasing skills, conflict management skills, and informative and persuasive public speaking competencies. When a typical introductory communication fundamentals course is over, both students and instructors have covered an astounding amount of information and skills; they may not, however, have a coherent vision of what is fundamental about human communication. They may finish the course viewing communication as a fragmented area of study and having little understanding of what is truly fundamental about how we make sense out of the world and share that sense with others.

The Solution

To help students remember and integrate essential information, we've organized the study of human communication around five fundamental communication principles. By synthesizing essential research and wisdom about communication, these principles provide a framework for understanding the importance of communication. They are designed to help introductory communication students see the "big picture"—the role and importance of communication—both as they sit in the classroom and as they live their lives.

Although the communication principles we highlight are included in some way in most introductory communication texts, they are not often used as a scaffolding to lend coherence to the entire course. In most texts, principles are introduced in the first third of the book and then abandoned, as material about interpersonal, group, and public communication is presented. We carefully discuss each principle in the Introduction following this Preface. Then, throughout the four volumes, we gently remind students how these principles relate to interpersonal relationships, group and team discussions, and public presentations. In other words, we cover classic communication content but organize it around five principles.

What are the five fundamental principles?

Principle One: Be aware of your communication with yourself and others.
Principle Two: Effectively use and interpret verbal messages.
Principle Three: Effectively use and interpret nonverbal messages.
Principle Four: Listen and respond thoughtfully to others.
Principle Five: Appropriately adapt messages to others.

A subtext of these five principles is the importance of communicating ethically with others. Throughout the volumes, in a feature entitled *Ethics and Communication*, we invite students to consider the ethical implications of how they communicate with others. We believe that, to be effective, a communication message must achieve three goals: It must be understood, achieve its intended effect, and be ethical. Our five communication principles for a lifetime are designed to help students realize these three goals.

The relationship among the five communication principles is illustrated with a pentagonal model. When a principle is introduced or discussed, the corresponding segment of the model is highlighted.

In addition to knowing the five communication principles, we want students to see how these principles relate to the classic communication contexts of interpersonal communication, group and team communication, and presentational speaking. We link the five communication principles with specific content by using a margin icon to identify a discussion of a skill, a concept, or an idea related to one or more of the principles. The icon, illustrated in the margin here, is explained in detail in the Introduction and appears in each volume to indicate applications of the five principles.

Overview of the Book

The text is organized into four volumes. In Volume 1, Chapter 1.1 covers the fundamentals, and then each principle is discussed and illustrated in a separate chapter. These chapters help students see the value of each principle and its centrality in their lives. Chapter 1.2 discusses the principle of being self-aware. Chapter 1.3 focuses on using and interpreting verbal messages. The emphasis of Chapter 1.4 is on using and interpreting nonverbal messages. Chapter 1.5 discusses the interrelated processes of listening and responding, giving special attention to the importance of being other-oriented and empathic. The last principle, appropriately adapting to others, is presented in Chapter 1.6; we use this principle to illustrate the importance of adapting one's behavior to accommodate to culture and gender differences among people.

Volume 2 links concepts and strategies for understanding interpersonal communication with our five communication principles. Chapter 2.1 helps students better understand the nature and function of communication in relationships. Chapter 2.2 identifies strategies that can enhance the quality of interpersonal relationships with others. Appendix A includes practical strategies for being interviewed and for interviewing others, relating interviewing skills to the five communication principles. Appendix B helps students balance the use of technology with interpersonal communication.

Volume 3 discusses how the five communication principles can enhance communication in small groups and teams. Chapter 3.1 explains how groups and teams work. Chapter 3.2 offers practical strategies for collaboratively solving problems, leading groups and teams, and running and participating in meetings. Volume 3 concludes with Appendix C, relating technology to group communication.

The final volume, Volume 4, presents classic content to help students design and deliver speeches, with references to contemporary research and the latest technological tools. Our popular audience-centered approach to developing a presentation emphasizes the importance of adapting to listeners while also being an ethical communicator. Chapters 4.1 through 4.5 offer information and tips on coming up with ideas for presentations, organizing and outlining messages, delivering presentations (using various kinds of presentational aids), crafting effective informative presentations, and developing ethically sound persuasive messages. Appendix D describes the use of technology in giving presentations. Appendix E includes two examples of recent presentations to illustrate what effective, well-planned presentations look like.

Special Features

A textbook is essentially a "distance learning" tool. When we write the book, we are separated by both time and space from the learner. To help shorten the distance between author and reader and engage students in the learning process, we've incorporated a variety of learning resources and pedagogical features. As noted in the text, information alone is not communication. Communication occurs when the receiver responds to information. Our special features help turn information into a communication message that can affect students' lives.

Principles Model and Icon   Our pentagonal model and margin icons help students see connections among the various communication concepts and skills we present. Throughout the volumes, we provide an integrated framework to reinforce what's fundamental about human communication. We want students to remember the five fundamental principles long after the course is over and they have forgotten the facts they memorized for exams. The principles can also help them remember strategies and concepts for enhancing their interpersonal relationships, improving group and team meetings, and designing and delivering effective presentations.

Principles for a Lifetime: Enhancing Your Skills   In addition to providing a margin icon to highlight text material related to one or more communication principles, we conclude each chapter with *Principles for a Lifetime: Enhancing Your Skills*, a summary of the chapter content organized around the communication principles. In Volume 1, these summaries distill essential information about the individual principle presented in a given chapter. In Volumes 2–4, we summarize the chapter content using all five communication principles for a lifetime as a framework. Miniature versions of the principles icon highlight the five fundamental principles. The purpose of this chapter-end feature is to help students integrate the descriptive and prescriptive information presented in the chapter with the five principles that provide the foundation for it.

Ethics and Communication   To help students apply ethics to what they learn about human communication, each chapter includes a feature called *Ethics and Communication*. In this revised and expanded ethics feature, we present a case study and then pose ethical questions for students to consider, asking them to ponder how they would respond to a specific ethical dilemma. The thought-provoking questions are designed to spark insightful class discussion or to be used in combination with a journal assignment or other learning method to help students see connections between ethics and communication.

Technology and Communication   Because of the importance of technology in our lives today, each chapter includes a feature entitled *Technology and*

Communication. This feature is intended to help students become sensitive to the sometimes mind-boggling impact of new technology on communication with others. The importance and role of technology are also discussed in several chapters throughout the volumes, as well as in appendixes to Volumes 2, 3, and 4. The prevalence of technology in students' lives gives rise to powerful teachable moments, which can be used to help students learn and apply communication principles.

On the Web   We do more than just talk about technology. By including Web resources that link to the topic of each chapter, we encourage students to reach out to the vast array of learning resources on the Internet. These annotated Web links provide background, context, and activities to help students apply course content.

Diversity and Communication   Each chapter includes a *Diversity and Communication* feature to help students see the importance of diversity in their lives. Yet we don't relegate diversity only to a boxed feature. Because diversity is such an important issue in contemporary society, we discuss it not only in a comprehensive chapter on the fifth principle of communication (appropriately adapting messages to others), but throughout the text as well.

Developing Your Presentation Step by Step   The chapters in Volume 4, Presentational Speaking, contain a series of boxes that follow one student's progress through the steps in preparing and giving a presentation. Students receive tips that they can readily apply as they prepare their own presentations.

Comprehensive Pedagogical Learning Tools   To help students master the material, we've built in a wealth of study aids:

- Learning objectives
- Chapter outlines
- Concise Recap boxes that distill key content
- Boldfaced key terms with definitions
- Chapter-end narrative summaries of the chapters
- Chapter-end summaries of the five communication principles
- Chapter-end questions for discussion and review
- Skill-building activities and collaborative learning exercises
- Practice tests

MyCommunicationLab   In this Portable Edition, you will find icons throughout each chapter that refer students to interactive materials available on this book's MyCommunicationLab (www.mycommunicationlab.com; access code required).

- **Watch** icons link to relevant and interesting video clips that supplement a topic being covered in the textbook.

- **Explore** icons link to activities that allow users to gain more knowledge of major topics in the book, reinforcing key concepts taught in the text.

- **Homework** icons link to assignments for students that reinforce material covered in the text.

- **Quick Review** icons link to practice tests that provide reinforcement of key concepts in the context of the book. These Quick Review assessments are not graded and give students an opportunity for self-study.

- **Visual Literacy** icons link to images that help illustrate important concepts.

- **Profile** icons link to relevant self-assessments, which enable students to test and evaluate their communication skills in different contexts.

In addition, the following tools appear in MyCommunicationLab (but not in the printed text).

- A **pre-test icon** appears at each chapter-level page. This icon prompts students to complete a pre-test before reading the chapter in order to gauge their prior knowledge of chapter contents. Results from the pre-test will be stored in the students' individualized study plans.
- A **post-test icon** appears at each chapter-level page. This icon prompts students to complete a chapter post-test after reading and reviewing the chapter content that will indicate a level of understanding of the chapter's material. Results from the post-test will be stored in the students' individualized study plans (see below).
- The results from the chapter pre-test and post-test generate a customized **study plan** for each student, identifying specific areas of weakness and strength. The study plan is organized by chapter and major topic area. Each time a pre-test and/or post-test is taken, the study plan is instantly updated to indicate which topic areas need to be reviewed. The study plan, as well as the pre-test and post-test, are for the students' use only and will not be shared with the instructor. This personalized study and review strategy allows students to track their progress in a topic and to prepare for their tests. This tool allows students to efficiently master the text and course material, save time studying, and perform better on exams.
- **MyOutline** provides students with the opportunity to create customized and specific outlines for their speeches.

In-Text Practice Tests In each chapter of the printed text, we've provided a practice test to help students simulate the test-taking experience. Written by Richard J. Sabatino, Texas State University–San Marcos, these practice tests are derived from the Study Guide that accompanies the main version of this text. Each test gives students the opportunity to gauge their comprehension of the chapter concepts. Answers to the practice tests can be found at the end of each volume.

Our Partnership with Instructors

A textbook is only one tool for helping teachers teach and learners learn. We view our job as providing resources that teachers can use to augment, illustrate, and amplify communication principles and skills. We also offer an array of materials designed for students, to enrich their learning experience.

Instructor Supplements

As part of our partnership with instructors to facilitate learning, we offer an array of print, electronic, and video resources to help teachers do what they do best: teach. Combined with the vast array of learning resources built into the text, this dazzling package of additional resources will help instructors forge both intellectual and emotional connections with their students.

- **MyCommunicationLab.** A place where students learn to communicate with confidence, MyCommunicationLab (www.mycommunicationlab .com) is an interactive and instructive online solution designed to be used as a supplement to a traditional lecture course or as a complete online course. MyCommunicationLab combines multimedia, video, communication activities, research support, tests, and quizzes to make teaching and learning more relevant and enjoyable. Students benefit from a wealth of video clips that include student and professional speeches, small group scenarios, and interpersonal interactions—some with running commentary and critical questions—all geared to help students learn to communicate with confidence. Access code required.
- **Instructor's Resource Manual** by Travis Russ, Rutgers University. For each chapter, the Instructor's Resource Manual provides at-a-glance grids that link text objectives to the manual's content as well as to other supplements. Additionally, each chapter includes an outline, discussion and journal questions, classroom activities and assignments, and Internet suggestions. Available electronically through the Instructor's Resource Center (www.ablongman.com/irc). Access code required.
- **Test Bank** by Sue Stewart, Texas State University–San Marcos. The Test Bank contains over 1,500 questions in multiple-choice, true/false, matching, fill-in-the-blank, short answer, and essay formats. Available electronically through the Instructor's Resource Center.
- **Computerized Test Bank**. The Test Bank is also available through Pearson's computerized testing system, TestGen EQ. This fully networkable test-generating software is available for Windows and Macintosh. The user-

friendly interface allows instructors to view, edit, and add questions, transfer questions to tests, and print tests in a variety of fonts. Search and sort features allow instructors to locate questions quickly and to arrange them in a preferred order. Available electronically through the Instructor's Resource Center.

- *A Guide for New Teachers of the Basic Communication Course: Interactive Strategies for Teaching Communication*, Third Edition, by Susanna G. Porter, Kennesaw State University. This guide helps new instructors teach an introductory course effectively. It covers such topics as preparing for the term, planning and structuring your course, evaluating speeches, utilizing the textbook, integrating technology into the classroom, dealing with challenges, and much more.

- *Blockbuster Approach: Teaching Interpersonal Communication with Video*, Third Edition, by Thomas Jewell, Bergen Community College. This guide provides lists and descriptions of popular videos that can be used in the classroom to illustrate complex concepts of interpersonal relationships. Sample activities are also included.

- *Great Ideas for Teaching Speech (GIFTS)*, Third Edition, by Raymond Zeuschner, California Polytechnic State University. This book provides descriptions and guidelines for assignments successfully used by experienced public speaking instructors in their classrooms.

- *Video Workshop for Introduction to Communication*, Version 2.0, by Kathryn Dindia, University of Wisconsin. Video Workshop is a way to bring video into your introductory communication classroom to maximize learning. This total teaching and learning system includes quality video footage on an easy-to-use CD-ROM, plus a Student Learning Guide and an Instructor's Teaching Guide. The result? A program that brings textbook concepts to life with ease and that helps students understand, analyze, and apply the objectives of the course.

- *Allyn and Bacon Digital Media Archive for Communication*, Version 3.0. This CD-ROM contains electronic images of charts, graphs, maps, tables, and figures, along with media elements such as video, audio clips, and related Web links. These media assets are fully customizable and can be used with the pre-formatted PowerPoint™ outlines or imported into the instructor's own lectures. The images are available for both Windows and Mac platforms.

- *Allyn and Bacon PowerPoint Presentation for Introduction to Communication*. This PowerPoint presentation includes approximately 50 slides that cover a range of communication topics: public speaking, interpersonal communication, group communication, mass media, and interviewing. Available electronically through the Instructor's Resource Center.

- *PowerPoint Presentation for Communication: Principles for a Lifetime*, Portable Edition, by James R. Smith, State University of New York, New Paltz. This text-specific package consists of a collection of lecture outlines and graphic images keyed to each chapter in the text. Available electronically through the Instructor's Resource Center.

- ***Lecture Questions for Clickers: Introduction to Communication,*** by Keri Moe, El Paso Community College. An assortment of questions and activities covering culture, listening, interviewing, public speaking, interpersonal conflict, and more are presented in PowerPoint. These slides will help liven up your lectures and can be used along with the Personal Response System to get students more involved in the material. Available through the Instructor's Resource Center.
- ***Communication Video Libraries.*** Adopters can choose appropriate video material from Allyn and Bacon's video libraries for Public Speaking, Interpersonal Communication, and Small Group Communication. Please contact your Pearson representative for a list of available videos. Some restrictions apply.

Student Supplements

We also offer an array of materials designed for students to enrich their learning experience.

- ***MyCommunicationLab.*** A place where students learn to communicate with confidence, MyCommunicationLab (www.mycommunicationlab .com) is an interactive and instructive online solution designed to be used as a supplement to a traditional lecture course or as a complete online course. MyCommunicationLab combines multimedia, video, communication activities, research support, tests, and quizzes to make teaching and learning more relevant and enjoyable. Students benefit from a wealth of video clips that include student and professional speeches, small group scenarios, and interpersonal interactions—some with running commentary and critical questions—all geared to help students learn to communicate with confidence. Access code required.
- ***ResearchNavigator.com Guide: Speech Communication.*** This updated booklet by Steven L. Epstein of Suffolk County Community College includes tips, resources, and URLs to aid students conducting research on Pearson Education's research Web site, www.researchnavigator.com. The guide contains a student access code for the Research Navigator™ database, offering students unlimited access to a collection of more than 25,000 discipline-specific articles from top-tier academic publications and peer-reviewed journals, as well as the *New York Times* and popular news publications. The guide introduces students to the basics of the Internet and the World Wide Web and includes tips for searching for articles on the site and a list of journals useful for research in their discipline. Also included are hundreds of Web resources for the discipline, as well as information on how to correctly cite research.
- ***Speech Preparation Workbook***, by Jennifer Dreyer and Gregory H. Patton, San Diego State University. This workbook takes students through the various stages of speech creation—from audience analysis to writing the speech—and provides supplementary assignments and tear-out forms.

- *Preparing Visual Aids for Presentations*, Fourth Edition, by Dan Cavanaugh. This 32-page booklet provides a host of ideas for using today's multimedia tools to improve presentations and includes suggestions for planning a presentation, guidelines for designing visual aids and storyboarding, and a PowerPoint presentation walkthrough.
- *Public Speaking in the Multicultural Environment*, Second Edition, by Devorah A. Lieberman, Portland State University. This booklet helps students learn to analyze cultural diversity within their audiences and adapt their presentations accordingly.
- *Outlining Workbook*, by Reeze L. Hanson and Sharon Condon, Haskell Indian Nations University. This workbook includes activities, exercises, and answers to help students develop and master the critical skill of outlining.
- *Study Card for Introduction to Communication.* Colorful, affordable, and packed with useful information, Pearson's Study Cards make studying easier, more efficient, and more enjoyable. Course information is distilled down to the basics, helping you quickly master the fundamentals, review a subject for understanding, or prepare for an exam. Because it's laminated for durability, you can keep this Study Card for years to come and pull it out whenever you need a quick review.
- *Introduction to Communication Study Site.* Accessed at www.abintro-comm.com, this Web site includes Web links to sites with speeches in text, audio, and video formats, as well as links to other valuable Web sites. The site also contains flashcards and a fully expanded set of practice tests for all major topics.
- *Speech Writer's Workshop CD-ROM*, Version 2.0. This interactive software will assist students with speech preparation and will enable them to write better speeches. The software includes four separate features: (1) a Speech Handbook with tips for researching and preparing speeches plus information about grammar, usage, and syntax; (2) a Speech Workshop that guides students through the speechwriting process and includes a series of questions at each stage; (3) a Topics Dictionary containing hundreds of speech ideas, divided into subcategories to help students with outlining and organization; and (4) a citation database that formats bibliographic entries in MLA or APA style.
- *Video Workshop for Introduction to Communication*, Version 2.0, by Kathryn Dindia, University of Wisconsin. Video Workshop includes quality video footage on an easy-to-use CD-ROM plus a Student Learning Guide. The result is a program that brings textbook concepts to life with ease and that helps students understand, analyze, and apply the objectives of the course.

Acknowledgments

Although our three names appear on the cover as authors of the book you are holding in your hands, in reality hundreds of people have been instrumental in making this book possible. Communication scholars who have dedicated their lives to researching the importance of communication principles, theories, and skills provide the fuel for the book. We thank each author we reference in our endnotes for the research conclusions that have led to our contemporary understanding of communication principles. We thank our students who have trusted us to be their guides in a study of human communication. They continue to enrich our lives with their enthusiasm and curiosity. They have inspired us to be more creative by their honest, quizzical looks and have challenged us to go beyond textbook answers with their thought-provoking questions.

We are most appreciative of the outstanding editorial support we continue to receive from our colleagues and friends at Allyn and Bacon. We thank Joe Opiela for helping us keep this project moving forward when we wondered if the world needed another communication book. Vice President Paul Smith has been exceptionally supportive of our work since we've been members of the Allyn and Bacon publishing family. Karon Bowers, Editor in Chief, has continued to provide valued support and encouragement. Our thoughtful and talented development editor, Carol Alper, helped us polish our ideas and words. Karen Black, Diana Ivy's sister, who conducted permissions research, was a true blessing, providing skilled assistance with important details and administrative support. We acknowledge and appreciate the ideas and suggestions of Mark Redmond, a valued friend, gifted teacher, and skilled writer at Iowa State University. His co-authorship with us of *Interpersonal Communication: Relating to Others* significantly influenced our ideas about communication, especially interpersonal communication.

We are grateful to the many educators who read the manuscript and both encouraged and challenged us. We thank the following people for drawing on their teaching skill, expertise, and vast experience to make this a much better book:

Lawrence Albert, Morehead State University
Leonard Assante, Volunteer State Community College
Dom Bongiorni, Kingwood College
Michael Bruner, University of North Texas
Jo Anne Bryant, Troy University
Cherie Cannon, Miami–Dade College
Diana O. Cassagrande, West Chester University
Dan B. Curtis, Central Missouri State University
Terrence A. Doyle, Northern Virginia Community College
Dennis Dufer, St. Louis Community College
Julia F. Fennell, Community College of Allegheny County, South Campus

Annette Folwell, University of Idaho
Thomas Green, Cape Fear Community College
Gretchen Harries, Austin Community College
Mike Hemphill, University of Arkansas at Little Rock
Teri Higginbotham, University of Central Arkansas
Phil Hoke, The University of Texas at San Antonio
Lawrence Hugenberg, Youngstown State University
Stephen Hunt, Illinois State University
Carol L. Hunter, Brookdale Community College
Dorothy W. Ige, Indiana University Northwest
A. Elizabeth Lindsey, The New Mexico State University
Xin-An Lu, Shippensburg University of Pennsylvania
Robert E. Mild, Jr., Fairmont State College
Timothy P. Mottet, Texas State University–San Marcos
Alfred G. Mueller II, Pennsylvania State University, Mont Alto Campus
Sara L. Nalley, Columbia College
Kay Neal, University of Wisconsin–Oshkosh
Penny O'Connor, University of Northern Iowa
Kathleen Perri, Valencia Community College
Evelyn Plummer, Seton Hall University
Kristi Schaller, University of Hawaii
David Shuhy, Salisbury University
John Tapia, Missouri Western State College
Charlotte C. Toguchi, Kapi'olani Community College
Beth M. Waggenspack, Virginia Tech University
Gretchen Aggert Weber, Horry-Georgetown Technical College
Kathy Werking, Eastern Kentucky University
Andrew F. Wood, San Jose State University
Debra Sue Wyatt, South Texas Community College

We have each been influenced by colleagues, friends, and teachers who have offered support and inspiration for this project. Happily, colleagues, friends, and teachers are virtually indistinguishable for us. We are each blessed to know people who offer us strong support.

Steve and Sue thank their colleagues at Texas State University–San Marcos for their insights and ideas that helped shape key concepts in this book. Cathy Fleuriet and Tom Burkholder, who served as basic course directors at Texas State, influenced our work. Tim Mottet, currently a basic course director at Texas State, is a valued, inspirational friend and colleague who is always there to listen and freely share his ideas and experience. Richard Cheatham, Dean of the College of Fine Arts and Communication, continues to provide enthusiastic encouragement for this project. Kosta Tovstiadi, from the University of Oklahoma, provided skilled research assistance to help us draw on the most contemporary communication research. Michael Hennessy and Patricia Margerison are Texas State English faculty who have been especially supportive of Sue's work. Finally, Steve thanks his skilled and dedicated support team at Texas State. Administrative Assistant Sue Hall, who continues to be Steve's right hand, is a cherished friend and colleague. Manuscript typist Sondra Howe and technical support expert Bob Hanna are two other staff members who provide exceptional support and assistance for this project and many others.

Ivy is grateful to her students, colleagues, and friends at Texas A&M University–Corpus Christi for their patience and unwavering support for her involvement in this book project. In particular, Michelle Maresh, Jason Pruett, Kelly Quintanilla, Flicka Rahn, Nada Frazier, Chair Don Luna, Deans Paul Hain and Richard Gigliotti, and Provost Sandra Harper constantly reaffirmed the value of a well-written, carefully crafted book—one that speaks to students' lives. Their support of Ivy's research efforts, along with constant "fueling" from her wonderful students, has made this project a real joy. Ivy's deepest thanks also go to Steve and Sue Beebe for their generosity in bringing her into this project, and for their willing mentorship.

Finally we express our appreciation to our families. Ivy thanks her ever-supportive family, parents Herschel and Carol Ivy, sister Karen Black (who supplied the permissions research and constant encouragement), and nephew Brian Black (whose humorous e-mails provided great comic relief). They have been constant and generous with their praise for her writing accomplishments. Ivy is especially grateful to her father, Herschel Ivy, for lovingly offering many lessons about living the highly ethical life.

Sue and Steve especially thank their parents, Herb and Jane Dye and Russell and Muriel Beebe, who taught them much about communication and ethics that truly are principles for a lifetime. They also thank their sons, Mark and Matthew Beebe, for teaching life lessons about giving and receiving love that will remain with them forever.

Steven A. Beebe
Susan J. Beebe
San Marcos, Texas

Diana K. Ivy
Corpus Christi, Texas

Communication Principles for a Lifetime

Underlying human communication are five principles that provide the foundation for all effective communication, whether we are communicating with others one on one, in groups or teams, or by presenting a public speech to an audience. We will emphasize how these principles are woven into the fabric of each communication context. The five communication principles for a lifetime are

Principle One:	Be aware of your communication with yourself and others.
Principle Two:	Effectively use and interpret verbal messages.
Principle Three:	Effectively use and interpret nonverbal messages.
Principle Four:	Listen and respond thoughtfully to others.
Principle Five:	Appropriately adapt messages to others.

These five principles operate together rather than independently to form the basis of the fundamental processes that enhance communication effectiveness. The model on the next page illustrates how the principles interrelate. The first principle, being aware of your communication with yourself and others, is followed by the two principles that focus on communication messages: Principle Two on verbal messages and Principle Three on nonverbal messages. The fourth principle, on listening and responding, is followed by appropriately adapting messages to others (Principle Five). Together, these five principles help explain why communication can be either effective or ineffective. A violation of any one principle can result in inappropriate or poor communication.

Principle One: Be Aware of Your Communication with Yourself and Others

The first foundation principle is to be aware of your communication with yourself and others. Effective communicators are conscious, or "present," when communicating. Ineffective communicators mindlessly or thoughtlessly say and do things that they may later regret. Being aware of your communication includes

Communication Principles for a Lifetime

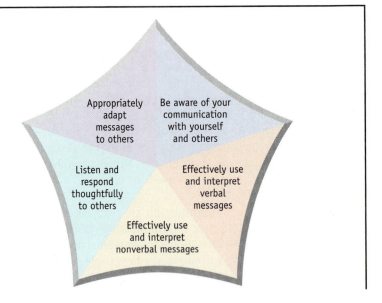

being conscious not only of the present moment, but also of who you are, your self-concept, your self-worth, and your perceptions of yourself and others. Being aware of your typical communication style is also part of this foundation principle. For example, some people realize that their communication style when interacting with others is emotional. Others may be shy.

Self-awareness includes being conscious of your intrapersonal communication messages. **Intrapersonal communication is communication that occurs within yourself, including your thoughts, your emotions, and your perceptions of yourself and others.** Talking to yourself is an example of intrapersonal communication. Although our intrapersonal communication is often the focus of psychologists, our intrapersonal messages also form the basis of our communication with others.[1]

Competent communicators are aware of the choices they make when they communicate both intrapersonally and with others; incompetent communicators react to others' messages with thoughtless, quick, knee-jerk responses. Because they do not mindfully censor themselves, they may blurt out obscene, offensive, or profane words. Ineffective communicators operate in an unthinking "default" mode. Being aware of our communication is a foundation principle because all of the choices we make when communicating rest on our ability to make conscious choices when we respond to others.

Human communication is the process of making sense out of the world and sharing that sense with others. Being aware of who we are and how we perceive, or "make sense" of, what we observe is a fundamental principle that helps explain both effective and ineffective communication.

Principle Two: Effectively Use and Interpret Verbal Messages

The second principle we introduce here is using and interpreting verbal messages effectively. Verbal messages are created with language. A **language is a system of symbols (words or vocabulary) structured by rules (grammar) that make it possible for people to understand one another.**

A symbol is a word, sound, gesture, or other visual signal that represents a thought, concept, object, or experience. When you read the words on this page, you are looking at symbols that trigger meaning. The word is not the thing it represents; it simply symbolizes the thing or idea.

Your reading skill permits you to make sense out of symbols. The word *tree*, for example, may trigger a thought of the tree you may be reading under now, a tree in your own yard or a nearby park, or a giant sequoia you saw on your family vacation in Yosemite National Park. Effective communicators use appropriate symbols to create accurate meaning. Author Daniel Quinn once commented, "No story is devoid of meaning, if you know how to look for it. This is as true of nursery rhymes and daydreams as it is of epic poems."[2] Meaning is created when people have a common or shared understanding.

The effective communicator both encodes and decodes messages accurately; he or she selects appropriate symbols to form a message and interprets carefully the messages of others. The process of using and interpreting symbols is the essence of how we make sense out of the world and share that sense with others.

Words have power. The words we use to describe ourselves and our world have considerable influence on how we perceive what we experience. Any good advertising copywriter knows how to use words to create a need or desire for a product. Political consultants tell politicians how to craft sound bites that will create just the right audience response. And words can hurt us. Words have the ability to offend and create stress. For example, derogatory words about someone's gender or race can do considerable harm. We will present strategies and suggestions for selecting the best word or symbol to enhance your listeners' understanding.

Principle Three: Effectively Use and Interpret Nonverbal Messages

Messages are also nonverbal. Nonverbal communication is communication by means other than written or spoken language that creates meaning for someone. Nonverbal messages can communicate powerful ideas or express emotions with greater impact than mere words alone. An optimistic hitchhiker's extended thumb and an irate driver's extended finger are nonverbal symbols with clear and intentional meaning. But not all nonverbal symbols are clearly interpreted or even consciously expressed. You may not be aware of your frown when someone asks if he or she may sit next to you in a vacant seat in a restaurant. Or your son may excitedly be telling you about his field trip to the fire station while you stare into the pages of your newspaper. You have no intention of telling your son he is not important, but your lack of nonverbal responsiveness speaks volumes.

One of the most important reasons our unspoken messages are significant is that they are the primary way we communicate feelings and attitudes toward others. With someone whom you like or love very much, you may spend a very small percentage of your time verbalizing your affection and friendship. The other person can discern your interest and admiration based on your nonverbal expressions and the amount of time you spend together. Your eye contact, facial expression, and tone of voice communicate your pleasure in his or her company. You may also know someone who doesn't like you. This less-than-friendly person may never have to come right out and say, "I don't like you." But you know you're not on friendly terms based on nonverbal cues: A scowl, an uninterested tone of voice, and a lack of eye contact signal that you're not held in high esteem. Our nonverbal messages communicate how we feel toward others.

When there is a contradiction between what you say and what you do, your nonverbal message is more believable than your verbal message. When asked how your meal is, you may tell your server that the meal is "great," but your nonverbal message—facial expression and tone of voice—clearly communicates your unhappiness with the cuisine. Our nonverbal cues often tell people how to interpret what we are saying.

Effective communicators develop skill in interpreting nonverbal messages of others. They also monitor their own messages to avoid unintentionally sending contradictory verbal and nonverbal messages. It's sometimes hard to interpret nonverbal messages because they don't have a neat beginning and ending point—the flow of information is continuous. It may not be clear where one gesture stops and another begins. Cultural differences, and the fact that so many different nonverbal channels (such as eye contact, facial expression, gestures, posture) can be used at the same time, make it tricky to "read" someone's nonverbal message accurately.

Principle Four: Listen and Respond Thoughtfully to Others

So far, our list of principles may appear to place much of the burden of achieving communication success on the person sending the message. But effective communication with others also places considerable responsibility on the listener. Because communication is a transactional process—both senders and receivers are mutually and usually simultaneously expressing and responding to symbols—listening to words with sensitivity and "listening between the lines" to nonverbal messages join our list of fundamental principles.

Listening can be hard because it looks easy. You spend more time listening than performing any other communication activity—probably more than any other thing you do except sleep.[3] Despite spending the greatest portion of our communication time listening, there is evidence that many, if not most, of us do not always listen effectively. What's tricky about listening? Both psychological, or internal, noise (our own thoughts, needs, and emotions) and external distractions (noise in the surroundings in which we listen) can create barriers to effective listening. The fact that it is perceived to be a passive rather than an active task makes listening and accurately interpreting information a challenge. Effective listening is *not* a passive task at all; the effective and sensitive listener works hard to stay on task and focus mindfully on a sender's message.

At the heart of this principle is developing sensitivity to others. By sensitivity we are not talking about the touchy-feely, emotional, what-I-hear-you-saying approach to interpersonal relationships. We are, however, suggesting that you develop an orientation or sensitivity to others when you listen and respond. **When you are other-oriented, you consider the needs, motives, desires, and goals of your communication partners while still maintaining your own integrity.** The choices you make in both forming the message and selecting when to share it should consider your partner's thoughts and feelings.

Most of us are egocentric—self-focused. We are born with an innate desire to meet our own needs. As we grow and mature, we develop a consciousness of more than our own needs. Scholars of evolution might argue that it is good that we are self-focused; looking out for number one is what perpetuates the human race.

Yet an *exclusive* focus on ourselves inhibits effective communication. Do you know anyone who is self-absorbed? Most of us find such a person tedious and uncomfortable to be around. People who are skilled communicators both listen and respond with sensitivity; they are other-oriented.

Principle Five: Appropriately Adapt Messages to Others

It is not enough to be sensitive and to accurately understand others; you must use the information you gather to modify the messages you construct. It is important to adapt your response appropriately to your listener. **When you adapt a message, you adjust both what is communicated and how the message is communicated and make choices about how best to for-**

mulate a message and respond to others to achieve your communication goals. Adapting to a listener does not mean that you tell a listener only what he or she wants to hear. That would be unethical. Adapting involves appropriately editing and shaping your responses so that others accurately understand your messages and so that you achieve your goal without coercing or using false information or other unethical means. To adapt a message is to make choices about all aspects of message content and delivery.

Regardless of whether you are giving a presentation, talking with a friend, or participating in a small-group meeting, as an effective communicator you consider who the listeners are when deciding what to say and how best to say it. One of the elements of a message that you adapt when communicating with others is the structure or organization of what you say. Informal, interpersonal conversations typically do not follow a rigid, outlined structure. Our conversation freely bounces from one topic to another. Formal presentations delivered in North America, however, are usually expected to have a more explicit structure—an introduction, a body, and a conclusion. The major ideas of a formal presentation are expected to be clearly identified. North American audiences also seem to prefer a presentation that could be easily outlined. Other cultures, such as those in the Middle East, expect a greater use of stories, examples, and illustrations, rather than a clearly structured, outlined presentation. Knowing your audience's expectations can help you adapt your message so that it will be listened to and understood.

You also adapt the general style or formality of your message to the receiver. If you are speaking to your lifelong best friend, your style is less formal than if you are speaking to the president of your university. The language you use and jokes you tell when around your best chums will undoubtedly be different than your language and humor when you are attending a meeting with your boss or with faculty members from your school. Our point is that effective communicators not only listen and respond with sensitivity; they use the information they gather to shape the message and delivery of their responses to others. Adapting to differences in culture and gender, for example, may mean the difference between a message that is well received and one that creates hostility.

Throughout the volumes of this book, we remind you of how these principles can be used to organize the theory, concepts, and skills we offer as fundamental to human communication. Chapters 2.1 and 2.2 will apply these principles to one of the most prevalent communication situations we experience each day—communicating with others interpersonally.

Understanding Interpersonal Communication

CHAPTER OUTLINE

CHAPTER OBJECTIVES

After studying this chapter, you should be able to

1. Define interpersonal communication and discuss its three unique attributes.
2. Distinguish interpersonal communication from impersonal communication.
3. Explain the difference between relationships of circumstance and relationships of choice.
4. Define interpersonal attraction and distinguish short-term initial attraction from long-term maintenance attraction.
5. Discuss three human needs that relate to complementarity in interpersonal relationships.
6. Provide examples of verbal and nonverbal ways we reveal our attraction to others.
7. Explain uncertainty reduction and describe three strategies of information seeking to reduce uncertainty.
8. Explain what is meant by the "art and skill" of asking great questions.
9. Describe some common verbal and nonverbal behavioral indicators of a self-absorbed communicator style.
10. Explain how one should give and receive a compliment.
11. Define self-disclosure and explain its role in relationship maintenance.
12. Discuss what is meant by reciprocity, appropriateness, and risk in self-disclosure.
13. Clarify ways in which self-disclosure and intimacy are affected by gender.
14. Identify and explain two models of self-disclosure pertaining to relationship maintenance.
15. Discuss how emotional expression, as a form of self-disclosure, affects relationship maintenance.

The best of life is conversation, and the greatest success is confidence, or perfect understanding between sincere people.

Ralph Waldo Emerson

Diana Ong, Sisy. © Diana Ong/SuperStock, Inc.

"Hi. I'm _____. Nice to meet you." This simple statement can strike fear in the heart of even the most outgoing individual. Yet we know that meeting and getting to know people, as well as becoming known, are some of the most rewarding experiences in this life. If we cannot break out of our comfort zones to communicate with others, we won't survive. As we said in Chapter 1.1, communication is inescapable. We communicate—intentionally and unintentionally, verbally and nonverbally—to accomplish things great and small throughout our lifetimes. And the most common, everyday kind of communication we accomplish comes in the form of simple conversations with loved ones, friends, coworkers, acquaintances, and even strangers as we go about our daily routines.

Think about your best childhood friend for a moment. Perhaps you're still in touch with that person; maybe that person is still your closest friend. But can you remember the very first time you talked to that person? Maybe something the person did contributed to your first impression. It's fun to try to remember and reflect on first conversations as we grow with others and progress in our relationships. If you're dating someone you've dated for a while or if you are married, think back to your very first conversation with your partner. Was it awkward? Was your first date so uncomfortable that you thought you'd never go out with that person again? Or was the conversation so engaging that you couldn't wait to see her or him again?

These elements are part of what we call interpersonal communication, the form of communication we experience most often in our lives. Interpersonal communication involves all five of our principles for a lifetime (see Figure 2.1.1). *In the remaining chapters of the book, you will see a small version of the*

Aware
Verbal
Nonverbal
Listen and Respond
Adapt

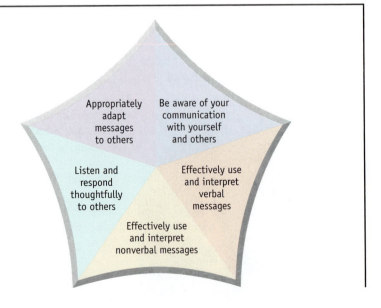

FIGURE 2.1.1
Communication Principles for a Lifetime

Appropriately adapt messages to others

Be aware of your communication with yourself and others

Listen and respond thoughtfully to others

Effectively use and interpret verbal messages

Effectively use and interpret nonverbal messages

communication principles model in the margin to highlight our reference to one or more of the communication principles that we discuss.

Effective interpersonal communication begins with an *awareness* of oneself. As you interact with people in your life, you make mental notes of what works well and not so well. You learn from these experiences and develop a personal style of communication. We continue this process by reassessing and reshaping our communication styles throughout our lives, with the goal of becoming better communicators. The second and third principles involve the *effective use of verbal and nonverbal messages.* We experiment with verbal and nonverbal communication as we interact with people, form relationships, develop those relationships, and, in some cases, let go of those relationships. A major element that enhances relationships is the ability to *listen carefully and respond sensitively* to others, our Principle Four. Finally, few interpersonal relationships last without *adaptation.* We live in an extremely diverse world. It's imperative to learn to adapt our communication to others—to their cultural backgrounds and values, personalities, communication styles, needs, and goals—so that we form satisfying relationships that help us enjoy our lives to the fullest.

In this chapter we examine interpersonal communication, distinguish it from other forms of human communication, and explore how interpersonal communication establishes and facilitates our relationships. As you work through this material, keep in mind those individuals who mean the most to you right now. Consider your communication with these valued people, assessing areas that are working well and areas that might need some attention. The more you personalize this information, the more you will gain from it.

What Is Interpersonal Communication?

In Chapter 1.1 we looked at three contexts in which communication most commonly occurs: interpersonal communication, group communication, and presentational communication contexts. In this chapter we explore the interpersonal context in more depth. To review the definition provided in Chapter 1.1, **interpersonal communication is a special form of human communication that occurs when two people interact simultaneously and attempt to mutually influence each other, usually for the purpose of managing relationships.**

Traditionally, interpersonal communication research has focused primarily on the face-to-face (FtF) encounter, as we have attempted to better understand how people use conversation and nonverbal cues to initiate and maintain relationships. However, given the immense popularity and general accessibility of the Internet, researchers are also studying interpersonal communication that occurs through this unique medium.[1] As our global society becomes more interconnected and we find we are able to "meet" all kinds of people worldwide through computer channels, it's important to examine how inter-

Early in a relationship, it's important to concentrate on listening to your partner's responses to your questions, so you can offer an appropriate follow-up response.

personal communication functions online. So, as we proceed through the various topics related to interpersonal communication, we explore how online communication is similar to and different from FtF interpersonal communication. As you read, think about your own relationships, both FtF and online, and consider how interpersonal communication facilitates each one. To begin, we consider three unique attributes that help us better understand the nature of interpersonal communication.

Interpersonal Communication Involves Quality

Imagine you're on a date and having dinner at a restaurant. The communication you have with your date is different from the communication you have with the person who waits on your table. (At least we certainly hope so; if not, you're probably having a lousy date!) Most likely, it is the quality of communication that differs.

Interpersonal communication occurs not just when we interact with someone, but when we treat the other as a unique human being. Conversely, **impersonal communication occurs when we treat people as objects or respond to their roles rather than to who they are as unique people.**

In fact, aspiring doctors are now required by the National Board of Medical Examiners to pass a daylong test of "bedside manner," revealing their ability to establish rapport with patients, ask clear questions, and listen effectively to answers. Until medical students pass the bedside manner test, they are not allowed to practice medicine. So they must learn to treat patients as people, using interpersonal communication skills, rather than as objects who warrant only impersonal communication.[2]

We engage in a good deal of impersonal communication each day. We may pass people on the sidewalk and say hello, whether or not we know them. The first few days of a semester are always interesting because of the presence of so many people new to the campus, so we may find ourselves giving directions to various campus buildings. Giving directions or instructions is a common yet important form of impersonal communication. Many people's jobs involve a great deal of impersonal communication. In the online context, an e-mail message to a friend is an example of interpersonal communication. Posting a message on an electronic bulletin board would be impersonal communication, since it is likely you would not even know the receivers of your posting.

Interpersonal Communication Involves Mutual Influence

Interpersonal communication also involves attempts at mutual influence. This means that both partners are affected by the interaction. We do not mean to imply that interpersonal communication exclusively involves persuasion—changing someone's mind or swaying someone's opinion. We simply mean that people who interact affect each other. For example, during dinner, you ask your date where he or she grew up, and you assume that your date hears you. If so, you've both been affected by the question—there's something you want to know and information your date can provide. But what if your date doesn't hear you? In this case, interpersonal communication has not really occurred between you and your date because there is no mutual interaction; only you have been affected by your attempt at communication.

"Harrison, it's time we had a face-to-face conversation — also known as *wireless communication*."

Every interpersonal communication interaction influences us. Sometimes it changes our lives dramatically, sometimes in small ways. Long-lasting interpersonal relationships are sustained not by one person giving and another taking, but by mutually satisfying communication.

Interpersonal Communication Helps Manage Relationships

Relationships are ongoing connections we make with others through interpersonal communication. For some people, the term *relationship* signals something serious and usually romantic. But we use the term *relationship* in a much broader sense in this text. You probably have a wide variety of relationships that include family members, coworkers, classmates, friends, and romantic interests. You may have some relationships that form and are maintained solely online. Many relationships involve a combination of FtF and online interaction.

We initiate and form relationships by communicating with those whom we find attractive in some way. We seek to increase our interactions with people we would like to know better, and we interpersonally communicate to maintain those relationships. We also use interpersonal communication to end relationships that we have decided are no longer viable.

Relationships form for different reasons. **Relationships of circumstance form situationally—simply because our lives overlap with others' lives**

in some way or because a situation brings us into contact. Relationships with family members, teachers, classmates, and coworkers typically fall into this category. In contrast, **relationships that we seek out and intentionally develop are termed relationships of choice.** These relationships typically include those with friends, lovers, and spouses or relational partners (such as gay and lesbian partners in committed relationships). These categories of relationships are not mutually exclusive. Relationships of circumstance can change into relationships of choice: Your sister or brother can turn out to be your best friend. Conversely, you may be extremely close to a certain family member, but over time that relationship becomes more distant and evolves into more of a relationship of circumstance than one of choice. Probably most of your relationships that involve online communication are relationships of choice. An online relationship of circumstance might be formed between members of a group, such as students enrolled in a class or employees of a company with several corporate locations, who interact through a listserv to discuss course topics or current projects.

We communicate differently in these two types of relationships because the stakes are different. Generally, relationships of choice are more important to us and central to our sense of well-being than relationships of circumstance. Also, we tend to be more intimate in relationships of choice, choosing to reveal more sensitive things about ourselves only with our closest friends or lovers. And with less intimate acquaintances or family members who have known us for some time we might "get away with" some behaviors that would be intolerable or a source of conflict within a relationship of choice.

RECAP

What Is Interpersonal Communication?

- Interpersonal communication involves **quality:** The quality of communication within interpersonal relationships is superior to that of communication that occurs impersonally.
- Interpersonal communication involves **mutual influence:** Both people in the relationship are affected by the interaction.
- Interpersonal communication helps **manage relationships:** Communication facilitates the initiation, maintenance, and, in some cases, termination of interpersonal relationships.

QUICK REVIEW

Initiating Relationships

Some people make relationships look so easy; they just seem to meet people and make positive impressions effortlessly. For others, meeting and getting to know people is a huge challenge. We'll let you in on a little secret: Initiating relationships really isn't all that easy for anyone. Let's begin our discussion of relationship initiation by exploring the nature of attraction—what draws us into a conversation in the first place.

Interpersonal Attraction: Why We Like Whom We Like

What does it mean to say that you are attracted to another person? Most of the time we tend to think of physical or sexual attraction. But there are many forms of attraction besides physical and sexual, including intellectual, spiritual, and personality attraction. **Attraction,** in general, **is a motivational state that causes someone to think, feel, and behave in a positive manner toward another person.**[3] More specifically, **interpersonal attraction is the degree to which you desire to form and possibly maintain an interpersonal relationship with another person.** Remember that interpersonal relationships imply some form of ongoing connection, so we're not talking here about those instances when you can't breathe because an incredibly attractive person walks by. Whenever we feel a positive regard for another person or when we like someone, we can say that we feel attracted to that person regardless of the sex of the person or our sexual orientation. However, the intensity of that attraction varies from relationship to relationship.

People use various forms of communication to convey their attractiveness to others and to form new relationships.

Interpersonal attraction occurs in both the early stages and the later stages of relational development. **Short-term initial attraction is the degree to which you sense a potential for developing an interpersonal relationship.** For instance, you might find one of your classmates physically attractive but never move to introduce yourself. Or you might interact with someone in a chat room and then decide that the person's comments attract you enough to begin private online exchanges. The information you gather in your first interaction with someone can generate a short-term initial attraction for a relationship, which you may or may not pursue, depending on the circumstances.

Long-term maintenance attraction refers to a level of liking or positive feeling that motivates you to maintain or escalate a relationship. It is the type that sustains relationships like best friendships or marriages. Short-term attraction gives way to long-term attraction as a relationship progresses. Rarely do you maintain a long-term intimate relationship, such as marriage, solely on the basis of what you initially found attractive.[4] You usually need something more as you develop an interpersonal attraction and deepen a relationship. Several factors come into play when you decide to act on your attraction and establish a relationship.

HOMEWORK

Similarity   Let's discuss the idea that "opposites attract." Opposites certainly do attract, and differences between people can be interesting. They can also form the basis for a good friendship or coworker relationship—after all, we learn a great deal from people who are unlike us. But we like to add another phrase onto the "opposites attract" cliché: "Opposites attract, but dramatic opposites seldom last." People who are opposites or significantly different in dispositions and preferences may intrigue each other and teach each other something, but they don't typically maintain a long-term relationship.

In general, you are attracted to people with whom you have **similarity— those whose personality, values, upbringing, experiences, attitudes, and interests are similar to yours.**[5] You may also be attracted more to persons who are similar to you in age, intelligence, and life goals. One of the most beneficial aspects of online communication is the unique structure of the Internet, which allows people with similar interests to find one another easily and form online relationships.[6] For example, new parents can find comfort in online chat rooms devoted to discussions of common experiences and predicaments in raising children. Interesting studies on dating partners and college roommates found that for both the partners and the roommates, similarity in the emotional dimensions of the relationship (such as comfort, ego support, conflict management, sincerity, and warmth) were more important than other dimensions of attraction and led to greater enjoyment of the relationship.[7]

Aware

In the initial stages of a relationship, we try to emphasize positive information about ourselves to create a positive and attractive image. We reveal those aspects of ourselves that we believe we have in common with the other person, and the other person does the same.[8] Think about your initial interactions with strangers, whether online or face to face; typically, you spend the first few minutes trying to find topics of mutual interest. You discover that the person is from a place near your hometown, has the same taste in music or sports, has the same attitude about school, and on and on. But the depth of this information is limited. You are likely to save your revelations about important attitudes and issues for later, as your relationship progresses. Attitude similarity is more

Ethics *and* *Communication*

The Harmless Crush?

Some years ago we came across a newspaper article that discussed flirtations or minor obsessions people have with one another, more familiarly known as "crushes."[9] One view suggests that crushes come in three sizes, "small, medium, and totally-ruin-your-life." However, many people extol the virtues of crushes, contending that "Crushes are great because they're harmless and limited in scope. They're little ego boosts. Even if you're already in a happy relationship, it's always nice to have someone paying attention to you." What ethical issues, if any, arise when someone who is in a monogamous romantic relationship feels physical and sexual attraction for someone other than his or her partner?

likely to be a source of long-term maintenance attraction than of short-term initial attraction.

Physical and Sexual Attraction   Volumes have been written about the role that physical and sexual attraction play in the formation of relationships.[10] While these forms of attraction are often lumped together or viewed as the same thing, they actually are different. In FtF situations, **the degree to which we find another person's physical self appealing represents our physical attraction to that person.** That appeal might be based on height, size, skin tone and texture, clothing, hairstyle, makeup, vocal qualities, gestures, and so forth. By this definition, even if you are heterosexual, you can still be attracted to a person of your own sex because you admire her or his physical attributes.

Nonverbal

   Is physical attraction a factor in establishing online relationships? Research reveals that many online communicators find the *lack* of emphasis on physical appearance and attractiveness in online relationships to be one of the most positive features of this approach to relationship development.[11] One set of researchers described the Internet as "a world where what you write, not how you look or sound, is who you are."[12]

   Sexual attraction has been defined as "the desire to engage in sexual activity with someone," a desire that "typically is accompanied by feelings of sexual arousal in the presence of the person."[13] You may be physically attracted to someone but not sexually attracted, as we stated before. But can you be sexually attracted but not physically attracted? We're not sure about the answer to that one because it may be a uniquely individual judgment. You may find another person's online communication sexually arousing, even if you've never seen the person in the flesh. Suffice it to say that these two forms of attraction usually operate in tandem, even though they represent different kinds of appeal.

   The adage "Beauty is in the eye of the beholder" is particularly true with regard to physical and sexual attraction. Each culture teaches and perpetuates its own definition of the physical ideal. In the United States, for instance, advertisements and TV programs promote a slender ideal for both females and males. This ideal contributes to the American obsession with losing weight and getting fit.[14] However, in some cultures, and at various times throughout U.S. history, physical attractiveness was synonymous with bulkiness.

   Our perceptions about others' physical attractiveness reduce relationship possibilities. In general, while we may be attracted to a range of persons, **we tend to seek out individuals who represent the same level of physical attractiveness we do.**[15] In nonverbal communication research, this is termed the **matching hypothesis.**[16] Perhaps you perceive yourself to be average looking, not model-beautiful but not unattractive either. You may be physically or sexually attracted to extremely good-looking people; but if you are average-looking, you are more likely to seek someone who is also average-looking to date, and even marry or become partners with. Look around the next time you're in a public place, like an airport or a mall, and notice the couples—

Diversity *and* Communication

What Attracts You?

Social psychologist Alan Feingold attempted to discover whether heterosexual women and men vary in terms of how much importance they place on physical appearance in the decision to date someone.[17] Looking for trends, Feingold reviewed a large number of studies on the subject and discovered that, indeed, men and women look for different things when deciding to initiate and develop heterosexual romantic relationships. Approximately 50 studies determined that men value physical attractiveness most in a potential partner, while women value personality, intelligence, kindness, sensitivity, and a sense of humor more than looks.

This information doesn't mean that heterosexuals are doomed because women and men look for and value very different attributes in each other. The sexes don't have to resent one another, claiming that men are superficial because they're drawn to looks while women are picky because they have "laundry lists" of qualifications for men. The information can be empowering, in that members of both sexes can understand and anticipate what attracts the other. Granted, there are exceptions; not everyone adheres to these sex-based findings on attraction. But in your experience, do men tend to emphasize a woman's looks over other aspects of her character? Do women prioritize psychological elements over physical ones in their interests in men?

people who obviously look like they are together. Most couples will match each other in terms of physical attractiveness.

Proximity   The principle of **proximity** in interpersonal relationships refers to the fact that **we are more likely to be attracted to people who are nearer to us physically and geographically than to those who are farther away.**[18] In your classes, you are more likely to form relationships with classmates sitting on either side of you than with someone seated at the opposite end of the room. Physical proximity increases communication opportunities, and opportunities to interact are likely to increase our attraction to those with whom we communicate. People involved in long-distance romantic relationships—those initiated through FtF encounters, but that evolve into long-distance, geographically separated relationships—understand the principle of proximity first-hand. They typically use multiple channels of communication to maintain their relationship, and the lack of proximity and accessibility to each other, over time, can become problematic.[19]

Social psychologist Sharon Brehm explains, "To meet people is not necessarily to love them, but to love them we must first meet them."[20] Of course, nowadays to "meet" someone need not refer to meeting someone physically. How many times have you heard someone say "I met someone on the Internet"? They didn't actually meet in the physical sense, but that meeting is just as real (sometimes more real) and valuable to those involved as FtF meetings. One line of research contends that proximity affects online relationships differently than it does FtF relationships.[21] The global presence and general accessibility of the Internet as a facilitator of interpersonal communication means that people can establish relationships even though they are geographically separated; without the Internet, they most likely would never "meet." But the instantaneous and pervasive nature of online communication bridges the physical distance, creating a virtual closeness that FtF relationships may not achieve. Thus the impact of proximity—a long-standing predictor of relationship development and success—is minimized in an online relationship.

Complementarity   While we tend to like people with whom we have much in common, most of us wouldn't find it very exciting to spend the rest of our lives with someone who had identical attitudes, needs, and interests. We may tend to be attracted to someone similar to us in important things like human values, but for other things we may be more interested in someone with whom we share **complementarity of qualities and needs—that is, persons with abilities, interest, and needs that differ from our own but that balance or round out ours.**[23] For example, if you are highly disorganized by nature (and that's fine by you), you might be attracted to someone who is very organized because you appreciate that person's sense of structure.

Social psychologist Will Schutz identified three interpersonal needs that motivate us to form and maintain relationships with others: inclusion, control, and affection.[24] **Inclusion is the need to involve others in our activities or to be involved in theirs. Control is the need to make decisions and take responsibility or the level of willingness to accept others' decision making. Affection is the need to be loved and accepted by others or the willingness to give love and acceptance to others.** Most people are attracted to those whose interpersonal needs complement their own.

If you have a high need to control and make decisions and a general disrespect or mistrust of others' decision making, you will be more compatible with someone whose need for control is minimal—a person who wants others to make decisions for her or him. Many committed couples reflect this pattern regarding finances. The person who is better at keeping track of bills and balancing the checkbook pairs

On the Web

How do people who are looking for romantic relationships meet other people? While singles bars and personal ads in newspapers are still around, people are turning increasingly to the Web to meet others. If you're interested in virtual dating, here are a few sites to try. (But be careful: Some services charge fees just to access the site and get started.)

www.eHarmony.com
www.Match.com
www.Matchmaker.com
www.eCrush.com

Here's some sound advice about Internet dating services.[22]

1. Browse the dating services to find one that will best suit you. Sites often focus on people with particular interests and profiles.
2. Do a free trial, if the site offers one, to see if you like the process before becoming a paying member.
3. Once you choose to invest time and money in a particular site, be as honest as possible in completing your profile. Don't describe yourself as you'd like to *think* you are; answer as you *really* are.
4. Provide a recent, realistic, yet flattering picture of yourself, even if you feel insecure doing so. You will receive more replies than if you choose not to include a picture (which can set off alarm bells in some people).
5. Don't be discouraged by responses you receive; it's typical to receive some rude or inappropriate messages from people whose motives are questionable.
6. If you do make a connection with someone and begin to exchange e-mail messages, pay attention to what is communicated, as well as what is *not* communicated.
7. If you decide to meet face to face with someone you've been e-mailing, be careful. Meet in a public place and have your own transportation so you can make a safe departure if need be. Make sure someone knows what you're doing, where you're going, and when you're meeting the person.
8. Once you meet, if you don't feel a romantic connection, don't be shy about telling the person you're really not interested. Be assertive and firm, but not rude, in expressing your desire not to pursue things further. No one likes to be strung along.

with someone who is good at maintaining a budget, to create a strong personal finance team. If you have high affection needs, you are likely to be less attracted to someone who is distant or aloof and who does not show affection. If you resent it when someone you are dating spends time away from you with his or her friends, you are likely to be less attracted to that person over time because you may have different, noncomplementary inclusion needs. In essence, we can view pairs of individuals as teams in which each person's needs complement those of the other person in some way. In reality, there are no perfect matches, only degrees of compatibility.

RECAP

Elements of Interpersonal Attraction

Short-Term Initial Attraction	This form of attraction involves a judgment that there is potential for an interpersonal relationship to develop with someone.
Long-Term Maintenance Attraction	This form of attraction is deeper and more long-lasting than short-term initial attraction and involves positive feelings that cause us to choose to maintain and escalate relationships.
Similarity	Attraction increases if our characteristics, values, attitudes, interests, and personality traits are similar to those of another person.
Physical Attraction	Attraction to another person's physical self.
Sexual Attraction	The desire to have sexual contact with a certain person.
Proximity	We are more likely to be interpersonally attracted to people who are physically close to us.
Complementarity	We may be attracted to someone whose abilities, interests, and needs differ from but balance or round out our own.

Communicating Our Attraction

In general, the more we are attracted to someone, the more we attempt to communicate with him or her. So the amount of interaction we have with someone indicates the level of attraction in the relationship.

When we are attracted to people, we use both indirect and direct strategies to communicate our liking, through nonverbal and verbal cues. **Nonverbal cues such as eye contact, forward lean, touch, and open body orientation that communicate feelings of liking, pleasure, and closeness are**

Nonverbal

typically indirect and are often referred to as immediacy.[25] Immediacy behaviors work to reduce the physical and psychological distance between people. For example, with people we are attracted to, we may sit closer, increase our eye contact and use of touch, lean forward, keep an open body orientation, use more vocal variety or animation, and smile more often than we normally do. Research also shows that individuals are more likely to preen in the presence of an attractive other.[26] For example, people may alter their posture to accentuate certain body parts, straighten or adjust their clothing, and fidget with their hair when interacting with someone they find attractive.

Most often we communicate our attraction nonverbally. But how do we let our online partners know that we're attracted to them? If the nonverbal cues that primarily communicate attraction in face-to-face encounters aren't available in online interaction, how do we communicate our interest?

One study asked almost 6000 people how they flirt in person as well as in online encounters.[27] The majority of people in the study reported that flirting was accomplished in relatively the same way, whether the exchange was face to face or online. They described how they translate physical actions into online text. For example, body movements such as laughing in response to someone's humor are represented by an acronym, such as LOL (for "laugh out loud"), placed in the text of a message or in response to one. Eye behaviors associated with flirting, such as a wink, are communicated through the use of emoticons (symbols formed with combinations of keystrokes to represent an expression or substitute for an action). Survey respondents explained that other indications of attraction, such as closer proxemics and touch, had to be accomplished through descriptions in the text of messages, such as saying "I wish I could reach out and give you a hug right now."

Verbal
Listen and Respond

On occasion, in both FtF and online contexts, we may communicate attraction verbally by using informal and personal language, addressing the person by her or his first name and often referring to "you and I" and "we." We ask questions to show interest, probe for details when our partner shares information, listen responsively, and refer to information shared in past interactions, in an attempt to build a history with the person. All of these behaviors demonstrate that we value what the other person is saying.

Getting That First Conversation Going

In some ways, online interpersonal relationships have an advantage over FtF relationships, in that they develop out of conversation, meaning that an online conversation is probably what launched the relationship in the first place. In an FtF situation, the process of noticing someone interesting, realizing you're interested (either physically, sexually, or interpersonally), finding a way to meet the person (either by introducing yourself or through a third-party introduction), and starting up the first conversation—all of these things can be nerve-racking. But these steps don't happen the same way in online interactions. Researchers have described online relationships as occurring in an "inverted developmental sequence."[28] Initial interactions are critical, in that they make

As online relationships grow more intimate, the partners' expectations for more emotional expression increase.

or break future online exchanges. Through repeated virtual contact, online topics of discussion often become very personal, and intimacy often develops at a more rapid pace than typically happens in FtF relationships. If rapport develops, it may lead to telephone conversations or FtF meetings.[29]

In FtF settings, once you realize you're attracted to someone (and that realization usually happens very quickly), what do you do next? That's a question that we've all no doubt asked ourselves at times, when we feel that awkwardness about wanting to find a way to meet someone we find attractive and get to know her or him. We have some practical suggestions for how you approach those first conversations, so that you feel confident and keep your self-esteem intact, while communicating effectively to impress the other person positively.

Reducing Uncertainty   Even though most of us like surprises from time to time, human beings are much more comfortable with certainty than with uncertainty. We prefer the known to the unknown, the predictable to the chaotic. Both FtF and online relationships involve uncertainty. One communication research team developed **uncertainty-reduction theory, which refers to a driving human motivation to increase predictability by reducing the unknown in one's circumstances.** It explains how we use information as we endeavor to reduce our uncertainty, especially as it relates to communicating with persons we don't know (or know well). Communication researchers Charles Berger, Richard Calabrese, and James Bradac contend that this driving motivation among humans to reduce our uncertainty prompts us to communicate.[30] We typically respond to uncertainty in three ways—using passive, active, and/or interactive strategies.

To illustrate these strategies, let's consider an example. You're at a social gathering with some friends. A lot of people are there; some you know, some you don't. You spot an attractive person across the room and decide that you would like to know more about him or her. What's the first thing you would likely do in this situation? Charge right over to the person and introduce yourself? Maybe some of us would, but most of us respond less actively at first to an uncertain situation like this. The first thing most of us would do would be to scope out the situation—see who the "object of our affections" is talking with, watch to see if he or she seems to be with anyone at the party, and casually observe how the person communicates to get some sense of her or his personality. These are all **passive strategies—noncommunicative strategies for reducing uncertainty by observing others and situations;** we seek more information in order to reduce our uncertainty. Passive uncertainty reduction is related to the first of the communication principles for a lifetime that we have discussed in this text: becoming more aware of yourself, your circumstances, and others.

After you've observed the person at the party, if you need more information before deciding what to do next, you might employ **an active strategy, which involves perception checking, or getting information from a third party.** You might ask your friends if they know the person, if he or she is dating anyone exclusively, what their opinions are about the situation or the person, and so forth. Finding out what your friends think of the person at the party increases your information and helps you decide how to behave.

The final approach, termed **an interactive strategy, is to go directly to the source who has the greatest potential to reduce your uncertainty.** In our example, an interactive strategy would involve actually going over to the person and starting a conversation or joining one in progress. In some situations, enough uncertainty can be reduced through passive and

Aware

Verbal

Technology *and* Communication

Gender and Online Communication

Do women and men communicate differently online? One study of online behavior found that men met more people online than women, and a greater percentage of men (77%) reported lying to their online relational partners than did women (46%).[31] Most of the lies were about age and physical appearance. While most of the participants described their online relationships as casual or friendly, more women than men reported forming intimate or romantic relationships online.

Another study examined how online relationships develop out of postings to Internet newsgroups.[32] Sampling approximately 700 newsgroups devoted to different topics, researchers surveyed online participants regarding their expressions of "real" versus "virtual" selves, the type of relationship formed from postings, the depth of the relationships formed, and actions taken online (e.g., sending e-mail messages) and in person (e.g., meeting face to face, having an affair). While men and women e-mailed, exchanged pictures, engaged in instant messaging, wrote traditional letters, and met in person with equal frequency as their relationships

developed, some differences emerged that mirror research results for FtF relationships. Women characterized their online relationships as being more intimate than men did. Women were more likely to express emotions and to self-disclose more and about more intimate topics than men in this study.

While gender differences are being detected in research, other scholars contend that the "online gender gap" is narrowing. As one team of researchers suggest, "conversing on the Internet may permit the user to step outside of constricting gender roles of communication and may allow males and females to communicate as equally robust and unfettered."[33] The view that more men use the Internet than women but that women are more likely than men to use the Internet to meet members of the opposite sex may be more myth than reality. As the Internet continues to become a more accessible, affordable, and acceptable forum for making new friends and exploring romantic connections, more men and women will no doubt experience the pros and cons of online relationships.

active strategies; there may be no cause for an interactive strategy. At the party, you may learn enough about the person you saw across the room by watching and talking to others about her or him that you decide against initiating a conversation.

Uncertainty reduction strategies aren't necessarily used in any particular order; you might bypass passive and active strategies and decide that the best way to cope with a situation is to get the information "straight from the horse's mouth." Interactive strategies are frequently used in online relationships, because starting up an online conversation or exchanging e-mails with someone tends to evoke less uncertainty than FtF first conversations. Online exchanges usually happen in private, with less potential for embarrassment than in FtF situations, when such factors as physical appearance and nervousness are in play.

But one element can inject uncertainty into the online situation: the potential for deception. Since you stare at a computer monitor rather than into someone's eyes when you "meet" online, you really don't know whom you're talking to. Research has shown people's tendencies to give false information or to omit pertinent facts in their online communication.[34] Subjects in studies reported lying about age, weight, details of physical appearance, marital status, and even their sex, meaning that some gender-bending experimentation certainly occurs. The uncertainty caused by the relative ease of online deception makes many a computer user gun shy about getting involved with people through the Internet.

RECAP

Strategies for Uncertainty Reduction

Strategy	Definition	Example
Passive	Observing and gathering useful information without interacting with anyone	While attending your first staff meeting at a new job, you observe colleagues and listen to their interaction, noting verbal and nonverbal behaviors in an attempt to "get the lay of the land."
Active	Getting opinions and information from third parties	As a form of perception checking, you ask colleagues their views on other coworkers. You compare their perceptions with your own observations.
Interactive	Getting opinions and information from those parties most directly involved	You ask the boss directly for her or his opinion and for information about the company and your job.

What Do You Say First?   In some contexts, the first words you exchange with someone may be fairly scripted or expected, such as in a job interview, in which introductions and ritualistic greetings typically take up the first few minutes. (See Appendix A for helpful information on communicating in interviews.) But what about situations in which there are no prescribed, explicit rules or expectations for behavior? Social situations, where you are meeting new people who may become friends or potential dating partners, create a level of anxiety for all of us—even the most confident person, who swears that he or she has absolutely no problem meeting new people.

Some interesting research has been conducted on just this kind of challenge. One study found that over 90% of college students surveyed agreed that it was just as acceptable for a woman to initiate a first conversation with a man as the reverse.[35] Students also believed that cute or flippant opening lines were less effective than an honest, direct approach. A book from the 1970s, entitled *How to Pick Up Girls!* provides some laughs today in its suggestions for opening lines men could use to start conversations with women.[36] Here are a couple of memorable ones: "You're Miss Ohio, aren't you? I saw your picture in the paper yesterday." "Here, let me carry that for you. I wouldn't want you to strain that lovely body of yours." "Haven't I seen you here before?" (and the all-time favorite from the 70s) "What's your sign?" We don't recommend the use of standard lines in opening conversations because that approach ignores the particular situation and the unique qualities of each person you will meet. Our fifth principle for a lifetime suggests that effective communicators adapt their messages to their listeners, so using the same type of communication in each new encounter is ill-advised. You should do some thinking about how you come across—and how you *want* to come across—when meeting new people.

One of the best strategies, whether in an FtF or an online situation, is to find something you perceive you might have in common with the person. In

Adapt

person, we all give off a certain amount of "free" information that others can easily observe. If someone is wearing a T-shirt from a place you recognize or have visited, or carrying a book from a course you've taken or are taking, you can use that information as a starting point for conversation. If your online conversation springs from exchanges in a chat room, you have the commonality of the chat room to rely on to get the communication flowing.

The Art and Skill of Asking Great Questions   When students ask us, as they frequently do, "What makes someone a good conversationalist?" a variety of things come to mind. All five of our principles for a lifetime could be reflected in our answer. But perhaps the most important element is the ability to ask a great question of another person. Research from the 1970s through the present shows that asking questions to generate conversation tends to be more of a woman's behavior than a man's.[37] However, men and women alike need to develop this skill so that communication in initial encounters isn't necessarily one person's responsibility and so that we don't perpetuate sex-role stereotypes. The ability to ask great questions doesn't just magically appear—it takes time, maturity, and experience with a variety of people and relationships to develop fully.

Adapt

Your conversational partners are likely to be impressed if you are able to show genuine interest and concern for them by learning to form great questions. What do we mean by "asking great questions"? We don't mean tossing rapid-fire, superficial questions at someone, as though you were in the first five minutes of a job interview. You don't want someone to think that you're gathering data for the census. Asking a great question means, first, tailoring the question to the person as much as possible. Use what you've observed and learned from other sources to formulate your questions. Online, it's typical to ask basic information just to break the ice, but the use of too many "yes/no" questions or questions requiring one-word responses doesn't advance the conversation. Avoid questions that might be too personal or probing in the early stages of developing FtF and online relationships.

Listen and Respond

A second, very critical skill to develop is to really listen to the person's answers to your questions. Then pose a follow-up question—one that is based on the person's response to your question. You can offer your opinion on something, but opinions work best when followed up with "Do you agree?" or "That's what I think, but what do you think?" Great conversationalists are great because they listen and then form responses that show they're listening—responses that are designed to draw other people out and let them shine.

Too many people think the best way to be conversationally impressive is by talking glibly, smoothly, confidently, and virtually nonstop *about themselves*. In an online context, when one person's messages are constantly five times as long as the other's and the content rambles on and on about the person, it's a definite turnoff. Terms for this behavior include **conversational narcissism (a communication style emerging from the view that one is the center of the universe)** and **a self-absorbed communicator style (a dominating communication style in which one focuses attention on oneself)**.[38]

Sometimes this approach to communication is an outgrowth of a personality trait. Other times it is a state, not a trait, meaning a temporary style of interacting rather than a more pervasive characteristic of a person. We can all be self-absorbed from time to time, but if the self-absorbed communication continues, if it moves from a temporary state into a more permanent trait, or style of a person, then the likelihood that the person will be positively perceived seriously declines.

Aware

You probably know what self-absorption sounds like and looks like in another communicator. Some verbal indications include the number of times a person uses the pronoun *I* instead of *you* or *we*. Narcissistic communicators converse mostly about themselves and typically provide more detail in their narratives than necessary (because they enjoy the sound of their own voices or the clicking of the keys on their keyboard).[39] They talk more in statements than questions and constantly try to top someone's story or to draw the topic of conversation toward themselves, as in "Oh, you think *you're* tired, let me tell you about the kind of day *I* had." No one's day is as bad, no one's opinion as valuable nor information as correct as the self-absorbed communicator's. The person may also feign empathy in a conversation: "Oh, I know exactly how you feel." This usually leads to "The same thing happened to me," followed by a long story that takes attention away from the original communicator. Another indication of self-absorption is evidenced in people who talk ad nauseam on topics about which they have some particular knowledge or expertise but that bore the socks off of listeners. Many times these types of communicators are driven by insecurity and uncertainty, rather than a belief that they truly are the center of the universe.

In FtF encounters, nonverbally self-absorbed communicators use vocal cues (such as increasing volume) and dominant body postures to hold their turns at talk and stave off interruptions from others. They may even physically block another person from attempting to leave the conversation and are generally insensitive to others' nonverbal cues. Online, self-absorbed chatters attempt to dominate the contributions of other chatters, make their postings more frequent and lengthier, and control the topic of conversation. People with self-absorbed personalities soon find themselves with few FtF or online friends, because few of us can tolerate such an out-of-balance relationship.

Nonverbal

So, in sum, the best conversationalists aren't great talkers, they're great listeners and responders (as we've articulated in Principle Four). In other words, it's not what *you* say, but how you respond to what *others* say that makes you a good conversationalist.

Listen and Respond

The Art and Skill of Giving and Receiving Compliments

Sometimes it seems as though people don't comment about one another unless it's to criticize. That's unfortunate, because positive reinforcement and support from others is central to our self-esteem. So let's discuss the lost art of the compliment. First, think about yourself: Are you a person who compliments others? If so, what do you tend to compliment people for—their appearance, hard work, scholarly achievement, athletic prowess? If you are a person who tends not to compliment others, why is that the case? Do you believe you'll be sticking your nose into others' business if you comment, even positively, about their behavior? Or are you somewhat oblivious to others, meaning that you tend not to notice what others do or how they look?

British linguistic scholar Janet Holmes calls compliments "social lubricants."[40] She explains that the most common purpose of a compliment is to make someone feel good by offering praise and encouragement, but an important byproduct is a sense of increased goodwill and solidarity between the complimenter and the receiver of the compliment. Research shows that compliments between romantic partners are viewed as a form of intimate talk, and that the sharing of positive feelings is linked to how satisfied partners are with the relationship.[41] In heterosexual relationships, women tend to be more aware of the presence and absence of compliments from their partners, although men and women equally believe that compliments are important in a relationship.

Verbal

Giving compliments is a tricky business, because some attempts at flattery can be taken in ways other than you intend. For example, many female professionals tire of receiving workplace compliments on their appearance while their male coworkers are more often complimented on their work-related achievements. Some compliments are too personal and can make people feel uncomfortable. A pattern of personal compliments may be grounds for a claim of sexual harassment. But these are extreme examples. We encourage you to think about complimenting as a communication skill and a strategy particularly useful in first conversations, whether online or face to face. You don't want to come across as a phony or a predator, but a well-thought-out compliment can open the door to further conversation.

Listen and Respond

It's also important to know how to receive a compliment graciously—not by agreeing with the complimenter (and sounding cocky) or by disagreeing or attempting to talk the person out of his or her compliment, as in "This old outfit? I've had it for years—I just threw it on today." The best response is a simple "thank you" that acknowledges that something nice was said about you.

Maintaining Relationships

Many forms of interpersonal communication are necessary to maintain successful, satisfying relationships. In this section, we explore a few of the most central forms, which represent some of the most heavily researched topics in the communication discipline.

Self-Disclosure: Revealing Yourself to Others

Imagine that you're on a first date. (If you have been married for quite a while, this will take some work, but try it anyway.) Things are going fairly well. You find that you like the other person, and you become more comfortable as the evening progresses. But while you're engaged in conversation, your date manages to turn the topic of discussion to sex. The person starts describing sexual details about his or her last date or romantic partner—information that is just too intimate and private for a first date or, by some people's standards, for *any* date. Have you ever been in a situation where your date told you "TMI" (too much information)? How did you feel about the person after that experience? Did the inappropriate disclosure stop the relationship from getting off the ground?

On a first date, we reveal less information about ourselves than we do after a more intimate relationship develops.

Self-disclosure, originally researched by psychologist Sidney Jourard, **occurs when we voluntarily provide information to others that they would not learn if we did not tell them.**[42] People can learn our approximate age, height, and weight by just observing us. But they can't learn our exact age, height, or weight unless we disclose it. Disclosing personal information not only provides a basis for another person to understand us better, it conveys our level of trust in and acceptance of the other person.

Reciprocity in Self-Disclosure   One thing we expect when we self-disclose is **reciprocity, meaning that when we share information about ourselves with other persons, we expect them to share information that is similar in risk or depth about themselves.** If you introduce yourself to someone and give your name, you expect that person to respond by telling you his or her name. If you reveal to someone online where you're from, you expect similar information to be revealed in the person's response. This cultural rule allows us to use disclosure as a strategy for gaining information and reducing uncertainty.

If the other person doesn't reciprocate, however, you might feel embarrassed or resentful. Sharing information about yourself gives others a certain amount of power over you. If the other person reciprocates and discloses similar information, it helps maintain an equal balance of power. But if one person shares information and the other doesn't, the resulting imbalance may cause discomfort. Over time, unreciprocated self-disclosure may cause someone to end a relationship.

Relationship experts John Harvey and Ann Weber describe relationship maintenance as "minding the close relationship," which they define as "thought and behavior patterns that interact to create stability and feelings of closeness in a relationship."[43] In a "well-minded" relationship, partners facilitate self-disclosure by questioning one another about feelings and behaviors, utilizing effective listener responses (such as head nods, eye contact, and vocal-

Verbal

Listen and Respond

izations like "uh-huh" when face to face or emoticons online), accurately repeating or paraphrasing their partner's disclosure, and remembering their partner's opinions and preferences.

Appropriateness in Self-Disclosure

Appropriateness is another key aspect of self-disclosure, related to the propriety of revealing certain information to another person. Certain kinds of information are inappropriate to disclose at an early stage of relational development but appropriate at a later stage. However, people vary a good deal on this dimension. It's sometimes hard to gauge what is appropriate to talk about and what is not while you're in the process of getting to know someone. Sometimes unwanted disclosures emerge because one person misjudges the nature of the relationship, assuming or wanting a greater level of intimacy than his or her partner assumes or wants.

Be sensitive to your partner when you choose what and when to disclose. Consider how the other person will react to the information. Although you may not think of some information as intimate, the other person may. Conversely, when your partner reveals information, try to determine whether it is highly personal to her or him. You could upset the other person if you fail to treat the information appropriately.

Adapt

Assessing the Risks of Self-Disclosure

Self-disclosure can be extremely rewarding because of its potential to deepen a relationship and enhance trust, but it is not without its risks.[44] For example, even in a society that seems to be becoming more accepting of homosexuality and bisexuality, "coming out of the closet" as a form of self-disclosure is still a very risky prospect. Relationships with family members and friends can be hurt at the revelation, and the potential for rejection of and hostility toward the discloser is very real.[45] When we disclose, we make ourselves vulnerable and forfeit control of information. We might hurt or insult the other person by saying things she or he finds offensive, signal an unintended level of intimacy, or damage the relationship with ill-timed and inappropriate disclosures. Typically, in relationships we seek a balance between the potential risks and rewards of disclosing personal information.

What is high self-disclosing for one person may be low self-disclosing for another. In judging what, when, and how much to disclose, it's important to realize that different people have different standards or expectations. For example, some individuals are quite comfortable talking about their personal problems with relative strangers, whereas others prefer such discussions only in the most intimate relationships, if at all.

Online and FtF relationships typically include periods of frequent self-disclosure early in the development process.[46] However, while the *level* of intimacy (or risk) in the information increases over time, the *amount* of disclosure tends to decrease as the relationship becomes more intimate. As a relationship proceeds, we share a good deal of low-risk information fairly rapidly, move on to share higher-risk information, and then, finally, to share our most intimate disclosures. The more intimate the relationship becomes, the more intimate

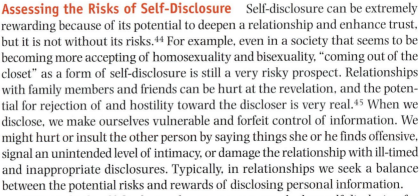

Verbal

the information that is disclosed. Holding back from sharing intimate information may signal a reluctance to develop a relationship.

Self-Disclosure, Intimacy, and Gender   Interpersonal communication research is extensive on the topic of self-disclosure and the development of intimacy in a relationship. But just what is intimacy? Experts use such terms as *bonding, closeness,* and *emotional connection* when referring to the sharing of personal, private information and experiences over time.[47] We especially like the definition developed by couples therapist Jeffrey Fine: "To be intimate is to be totally transparent, emotionally naked in front of another who is equally transparent. You want to see into the other's heart. What people should mean when they say *intimacy* is in-to-me-see."[48]

The conventional wisdom, borne out by early studies, contends that relationships cannot fully develop into intimacy unless both partners share (ideally, with equal frequency and depth) information about themselves.[49] Without self-disclosure, we form only superficial relationships. However, research on gender and self-disclosure calls the conventional wisdom and prior findings into question.[50]

Verbal

Consider for a moment men's friendships with other men. Think about golfing buddies, a group of guys who gather over lunch a few times a week to shoot some hoops, or men who enjoy one another's company over a few beers. Do these relationships tend to be based on an intimate sharing of personal information? Or are they based on shared experiences, on doing things together or having interests in common? Now think about how women's friendships form, in general. Do they form more through shared activities or through communication? It's not a stereotype: Women's friendships with other women *are* more often developed through interpersonal communication, particularly self-disclosure, than through common experiences.[51]

So, if men's friendships tend to form on the basis of shared activities, are they any less meaningful than relationships that develop through communication? Research has attempted to discover what constitutes intimacy for men, how men's friendships form, and what makes them meaningful.[52] Most men describe their friendships with other men as forming quite differently than their friendships with women, but being just as satisfying and important.[53] Men's friendships more often develop by doing, while relationships with female friends involve more talking. Men who experience the terror of battle together form powerful bonds, developed from shared experience rather than shared

On the Web

Does self-disclosure, as a tool for enhancing intimacy in relationships, operate the same way in cyberspace as it does face to face? Apparently, according to research on Internet usage, people are telling other people all kinds of things about themselves over the Net. Revealing personal information about oneself isn't as threatening to many people when accomplished through machines to someone in another location, rather than in face-to-face encounters. What's your view of self-disclosure and relationship development in cyberspace? Have you shared personal information with an online partner, or has someone shared personal information with you? If you haven't, but you're daring enough to try, here are a couple of sites to check out:

www.love.com, created by America Online, contains close to 200,000 personal ads. Chat rooms at this site serve as meeting places and arenas for exploring relationships. If you are a member of AOL, you also have access to their site Love@AOL.[54]

luvcoach@aol.com is the site of Robert Bruce Starr, known as the "Luvcoach" at America Online. He opens his chat room, called "Relationship Coaching," a few times a week and gives relationship advice to computer users. Users also chat with each other about a wide variety of relational issues.[55]

personal information down in the trenches. To suggest that only superficial relationships can be accomplished by doing, while deep ones must be accomplished by communicating, is to measure relational intimacy with a feminine yardstick.[56]

Self-Disclosure

. . . is providing someone with information about yourself that she or he couldn't learn about you unless you revealed it.

. . . should be reciprocal, meaning that the person you reveal something to should respond with information about himself or herself that is similar in depth. The frequency with which partners self-disclose should be reciprocal as well.

. . . should be appropriate, meaning that it can be a mistake to reveal information that is too personal too soon in the development of a relationship.

. . . involves some risk, because knowledge is power. By revealing information to another person, you give that person a degree of power over you.

. . . is highly rewarding, in that it is a building block of relational intimacy.

Two Models of Self-Disclosure

Research has explored the way in which self-disclosure works to move a relationship toward intimacy. Here, we examine two of the more prominent models that illustrate the process by which this happens.

The Social Penetration Model   A pair of researchers, Irwin Altman and Dalmas Taylor, developed a model that illustrates how much and what kind of information we reveal in various stages of a relationship.[57] **Social penetration is a model of self-disclosure that asserts that both the breadth and the depth of information shared with another person increase as the relationship develops.** According to their theory, interpersonal communication in relationships moves gradually from the superficial to the more intimate.

Their model is a configuration of rings, or concentric circles (see Figure 2.1.2). The outermost circle represents breadth, or all the potential information about yourself that you could disclose to someone—information about athletic activities, spirituality, family, school, recreational preferences, political attitudes and values, and fears. Then there are a series of inner circles, which represent the depth of information you could reveal about yourself. The innermost circle represents your most personal information.

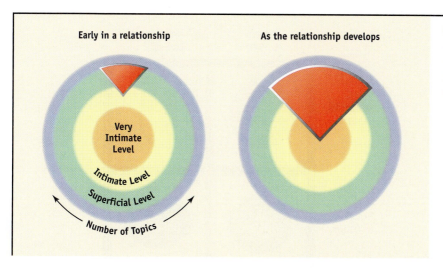

FIGURE 2.1.2
Altman and Taylor's Concentric Circles and Wedge of Social Penetration

As an online or FtF relational partner interacts with you, that interaction can be seen as a wedge that is at first narrow (few topics are discussed) and shallow (topics are fairly superficial). People who have just started dating might talk about commonalities (like being students at the same college), hobbies, interests, and favorite activities. As the relationship progresses, the wedge becomes broader (as more topics are discussed) and deeper (as more personal topics are discussed). After several dates or conversations about hobbies and interests, topics might turn more to values, like the importance of family and friendships or attitudes about politics or social issues. Self-disclosure causes your layers to be penetrated, as you penetrate the layers of the other person.

Each of your relationships exhibits a certain degree of social penetration, or the extent to which the other person has entered your concentric circles. Some relationships, such as those with professors, distant family members, and acquaintances, may reflect a narrow, shallow wedge. The relationship does not involve a great deal of personal disclosure. A few relationships represent almost complete social penetration, the kind you achieve in an intimate, well-developed relationship, in which a large amount of in-depth self-disclosure has occurred. But many contend that no one can ever completely know another person; there may be no such thing as complete social penetration. This model is a helpful way to assess your relationships, in terms of who you allow or encourage to get close to you and why. It may also help you diagram the level of intimacy you have in online and FtF relationships with others, as you attempt to penetrate their layers.

The Johari Window   **The Johari Window** in Figure 2.1.3 **is another model of how self-disclosure varies from relationship to relationship. It reflects various stages of relational development, degrees of self-awareness, and others' perceptions of us.** Its name comes from the first

Aware

FIGURE 2.1.3
Johari Window

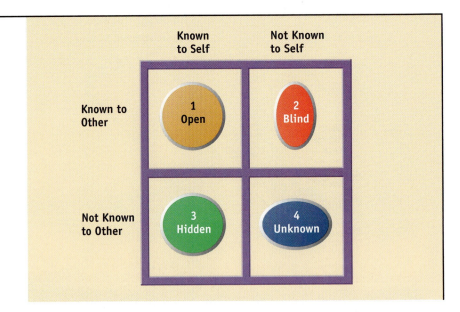

names of the two men who developed it (Joe Luft and Harry Ingham) and from its windowlike appearance.[58] The square window, like the circles in the social penetration model, represents your self. This self encompasses everything about you, including things you don't see or realize. A vertical line divides the square into what you have come to know about yourself and what you don't yet know about yourself. A horizontal line divides the square into what another person knows about you and doesn't know about you. The intersection of these lines creates a four-paned window.

The *Open* quadrant represents that part of yourself that you know and have revealed to the other person. As a relationship becomes more intimate, the Open quadrant grows larger. The *Hidden* quadrant is information you know about yourself but have not shared with the other person. This quadrant is fairly large initially; but, as you self-disclose, it shrinks, and the Open quadrant grows. The information in the *Unknown* quadrant is that part of yourself that you have yet to discover or realize. As you learn and self-disclose more, or as others learn more about you, this quadrant becomes smaller. Individuals who are not very introspective and do not have a very well-developed sense of self will have larger Unknown areas than those who have made a concerted effort to come to know themselves.

Sometimes our friends observe things about us that we don't realize or perceive about ourselves. This kind of unintentional self-disclosure is represented by the *Blind* quadrant. This quadrant includes real aspects of ourselves that we fail to recognize. The Blind quadrant is usually small when someone doesn't know us very well; it grows larger as that person observes more information that is in our Unknown quadrant. However, as the relationship becomes more intimate, the other person is more likely to reveal his or her perceptions of us, so the Unknown and the Blind quadrants shrink as the information becomes known and accessible to us. As you can see, then, intimate relationships play an important role in the growth of self-knowledge.

Expressing Emotions

Expressing emotions is another powerful way we reveal ourselves to others and deepen our relationships. Such expression comes more easily to some people than others, but it is a skill that can be improved in both your online and your FtF relationships.[59] However, there are cultural barriers to achieving this skill, in that many cultures designate particular emotions as appropriate for only some people to display in certain situations.[60] If you placed emotional expression on a continuum according to cultural groups, with one end being an open approach to emotional display and the other end being the suppression of emotional display, U.S. culture would fall somewhere in the middle. Some cultural groups (such as Latin cultures) are comfortable with and accepting of emotional display, while other groups (such as Asian cultures) value emotional inhibition more than people in the United States.[61] People from countries where the norm is emotional inhibition often think that Americans "wear their hearts on their sleeves," while people from some other cultures view Americans as being "pent up" emotionally.

Families teach children very specific rules about the appropriateness of emotional display. One fascinating nonverbal communication study found that, at very young ages, children learn to mask disappointment in order to be

Nonverbal

Some researchers believe that many men are drawn to sports because the sporting event allows them emotional release that might be considered inappropriate in other contexts.

socially appropriate.[62] We also perpetuate gender distinctions regarding emotions.[63] Many American men are taught to contain their emotions for fear that emotional expression may make them appear weak. Acquiring a "poker face" is a goal. Men are allowed to show anger and jealousy (short of physical violence), but it is frowned on for men to reveal sadness, fear, or great joy—unless they reveal it in a sporting context. (Some believe that this is one reason so many men are drawn to sports; the sporting context allows them emotional release that would most likely be considered inappropriate or "unmanly" in other contexts.) In fact, the male tendency to suppress emotion is so pronounced, it led Sidney Jourard (who first studied self-disclosure) to entitle one of his book chapters, "The Lethal Aspects of the Male Role."[64] Jourard found that men who had difficulty expressing their feelings had high levels of stress-related disease. Research suggests that if and when men do disclose their feelings to someone, most seek women as listeners because they report feeling safer expressing emotions to women than to other men.[65]

Women in American culture, in most settings, are allowed the emotional display of crying that can be prompted by sadness, fear, or joy. (Exceptions include some professional settings, where "keeping one's cards close to the vest" is valued and displaying emotion is deemed inappropriate.) But many women receive negative reactions when they display anger. The view persists that an angry woman is "out of control" or "hormonal," while an angry man is behaving more in line with societal expectations for members of his sex. While these trends and expectations have changed somewhat with recent generations, there is still a significant tendency for men (and many women as well) to believe that emotional expression of any kind is more appropriate in women than men.[66]

Many of us are reluctant or embarrassed to talk about our feelings or show our emotions, yet expressing feelings is a primary way we develop and deepen our relationships. We share feelings with our partners in two primary ways. First, we disclose more indirectly information about our past and current emotional states and experiences, such as sadness about the death of a family member or fear about what we will do after we graduate. This form of disclosure is more common in a growing relationship. The second way is the direct expression of emotions such as expressing attraction, love, or disappointment toward our partners. This form typically emerges later in the development of a relationship.[67]

As relationships become more intimate, we have a greater expectation that our partner will disclose emotions openly. The amount of risk associated with such emotional disclosure varies from person to person. Most of us are comfortable sharing positive emotions such as happiness and joy but are more reserved about sharing negative emotions such as fear or disappointment. In a study of 46 committed, romantic couples, subjects reported that the number-one problem in their relationship was an inability to talk about negative feelings.[68] For example, partners often made the following types of observations: "When she gets upset, she stops talking"; "He never lets me know when he's upset with something he doesn't like"; and "He just silently pouts." We generally want to know how our partners in intimate relationships are feeling, even if those feelings are negative.[69]

WATCH

Verbal

QUICK REVIEW

PRINCIPLES FOR A LIFETIME: Enhancing Your Skills

Principle One: Be aware of your communication with yourself and others.

- Attraction emerges in several different forms; it's important to discover what traits in other persons are attractive to you.
- Early in an online or FtF relationship, be aware of aspects of your personality that you want to emphasize to another person in order to create a positive and attractive image.
- One strategy to reduce uncertainty in interpersonal contexts is to be aware of your surroundings and situation as you passively observe others' interactions.
- The Johari Window is a model that can help you become more aware of your relationships and your interpersonal communication.

Aware

Principle Two: Effectively use and interpret verbal messages.

- In initial interactions, honest, direct approaches are preferable to "canned" opening lines.
- When initiating online or FtF relationships, use questions that will engage and draw out another person.
- You may verbally reveal your liking for another person by using informal, personal, and inclusive language.
- You may verbally reveal your liking for another person by asking questions, probing for further information, and directly expressing your feelings.
- An active strategy to reduce uncertainty in interpersonal contexts is to ask third parties for their perceptions and knowledge.
- An interactive information-seeking strategy involves direct communication with the source who has the greatest potential for reducing your uncertainty.
- Asking great questions in a conversation draws a person out and helps a communicator avoid creating a perception of being self-absorbed.
- Practice giving sincere compliments generously and receiving others' compliments graciously.
- One of the key variables in relationship development is self-disclosure.
- As relationships grow more intimate, the expectation for deeper, more personal self-disclosure increases.
- Women's relationships tend to rely more on verbal communication, especially self-disclosure, while men's relationships with other men more often develop out of shared activities or common experiences.
- As online and FtF relationships grow more intimate, the expectation for more emotional expression increases.

Verbal

Principle Three: Effectively use and interpret nonverbal messages.

- Physical attraction is the degree to which you find another person's physical self appealing, while sexual attraction is the desire to have sexual contact with a certain person.
- In an FtF relationship, you may nonverbally reveal your liking for another person through the display of immediacy cues.
- In an online relationship, acronyms and emoticons help convey interest.
- Certain nonverbal behaviors, such as increasing the volume of your voice to keep someone from interrupting you or posting multiple, lengthy messages in a chat rooom, can signal a self-absorbed style of interpersonal communication.

Nonverbal

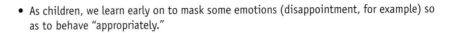

- As children, we learn early on to mask some emotions (disappointment, for example) so as to behave "appropriately."

Principle Four: Listen and respond thoughtfully to others.

Listen and Respond

- Early in online and FtF relationships, it's important to concentrate on and listen to your partner's responses to your questions, so you can offer an appropriate follow-up response.
- You may verbally reveal your attraction and liking for other people by listening, asking questions to elicit more detail, and then responding appropriately and sensitively to the added information.
- The best conversationalists aren't great talkers, they're great listeners and responders.
- The formulation of great questions in conversation requires listening carefully and responding appropriately to someone's communication.
- It's important to attend carefully to someone's self-disclosure, because it comes with an expectation of reciprocity, meaning that a receiver is expected to self-disclose in response to a sender's self-disclosure.

Principle Five: Appropriately adapt messages to others.

Adapt

- Adapt to others' communication, especially in first conversations, by attending to what is said and following up with great questions.
- A self-absorbed style of communication involves very little adaptation to others.
- Adapt your self-disclosure to the other person and the context, so that your revelations are appropriate.

SUMMARY

In this chapter we explored the important topic of interpersonal communication—the form of communication that we use most frequently in our lives. Effective interpersonal communication is intricately related to one's ability to enact the five communication principles for a lifetime. We first defined interpersonal communication as a special form of human communication that occurs when we interact with another person and attempt to mutually influence each other, usually for the purpose of managing online or FtF relationships. We then differentiated interpersonal communication from impersonal communication and relationships of circumstance from relationships of choice.

We all know that relationships are important, but just how do they begin? In this chapter we explored the concept of attraction in its various forms, distinguishing interpersonal attraction as the form that causes us to forge ongoing connections with others. Four primary factors play a role in interpersonal attraction, including how similar we perceive ourselves to be to our relational partners, how physically and/or sexually attracted we are to them, our proximity to them, and whether our personality traits, values, and needs are complementary to theirs. We explored ways that we verbally and nonverbally communicate our attraction to others, as we attempt to form friendships, relationship with coworkers, romances, and committed partnerships.

Once you acknowledge that you are attracted to another person and desire a relationship with her or him, how do you use communication to get that relationship off the ground? Whether our relationships form online or in person, most of us face a degree of uncertainty when meeting new people. We attempt to reduce that uncertainty by seeking information in passive, active, and/or interactive ways. We then must call on our best communication skills to get to know the other person. Rather than communicating about ourselves in a self-absorbed or narcissistic fashion, it is better to learn to ask questions of the other person that will draw him or her out and get a conversation going. Learning to give and receive compliments graciously and sincerely is a skill we can all benefit from, because the compliment is a unique form of interpersonal communication that can have a profoundly positive effect on a relationship.

One of the most important forms of interpersonal communication that facilitates our online and FtF relationships is self-disclosure, defined as revealing something about ourselves to another person that she or he would not otherwise know if we did not reveal it. The rate and depth of self-disclosure vary as a relationship progresses, but we expect self-disclosure to be reciprocal. This means that if we share something about ourselves, we expect our partners to respond in kind, both in frequency and depth of information. Self-disclosure is also expected to be appropriate to the level of intimacy of the relationship. And self-disclosing involves a degree of risk.

One way to develop intimacy in a relationship is to disclose personal information, but research has determined that self-disclosure is not the only road to intimacy. Gender affects how one develops relationships, in that men may develop close friendships with other men more through shared activities than through shared information. Women, on the other hand, are more likely to deepen relationships by disclosing information than by sharing an experience. We discussed two models of self-disclosure: the social penetration model, which focuses on how one's personal layers are revealed to others; and the Johari Window, which illustrates self-awareness and relational partners' perceptions of us. Another form of disclosure is the expression of emotions to relational partners. The degree to which we feel safe discussing or displaying our emotions to others is a measure of intimacy in a relationship.

DISCUSSION AND REVIEW

1. Why is interpersonal communication important in our lives?

2. What three components make up the definition of interpersonal communication?

3. Discuss three forms of attraction explained in this chapter. Then explore ways in which we verbally and nonverbally communicate our attraction for others.

4. What are the three basic interpersonal needs, according to Will Schutz, whose research we reviewed in this chapter? How does the concept of

complementarity in a relationship relate to these three needs?

5. Discuss uncertainty-reduction theory in the context of online and FtF interpersonal relationships. What three information-seeking strategies do we typically use to reduce our uncertainty?

6. We've all met people who were self-absorbed or who exhibited self-absorbed communication styles. Explain, first, what is meant by self-absorption in interpersonal communication; then provide some examples that illustrate this style.

7. What is a "great" question? Provide examples of great questions that could be used to initiate conversations and relationships with others.

8. What is self-disclosure and how does it function to develop intimacy in a relationship?

9. What does the social penetration model teach us about relationship development?

10. Explain how the Johari Window reveals our view of self, as well as others' views of us. In what ways could the Johari Window be helpful in the assessment of our relationships?

PUTTING PRINCIPLES INTO PRACTICE

1. Using a model of concentric circles, map out your interpersonal relationships. Put your name in the core circle, then write the names of those persons closest to you on the circle closest to the core, continuing outward and noting the names of those with whom you have personal relationships according to intimacy. Note whether these are FtF or online relationships, or a combination of the two. Once you have completed your model, think about how your communication differs with people on the innermost circles versus those on the outermost circles. What kind of communication is required to move someone from an outer circle to an inner one; in other words, how do you communicate in order to increase closeness or intimacy with someone? Do you ever sense a need to "lighten up" with someone on an inner ring, possibly moving them to an outer ring? How do you use interpersonal communication to accomplish this?

2. Think about someone to whom you are now or once were extremely attracted. Assess that attraction by considering these questions: How similar were you to that person, in terms of temperament, values, personality, and interests? Was your attraction to that person physical? Sexual? Intellectual? Psychological (meaning an attraction to his or her personality)? Spiritual? A combination of some of these? What kind of proximity did you have to the person? Did you have ready access to him or her? If not, what kind of effect did that have on your attraction? How complementary were your abilities and needs?

3. With a group of classmates, generate lists of the worst opening lines you can think of for getting a first conversation off the ground. Then discuss the use of canned opening lines as a strategy for initiating conversation. Should these types of lines be used? If someone uses a standard line to start a conversation, what happens to the ability to adapt one's communication to one's listeners?

4. Because we think that learning to ask great questions is so important, we want to provide you an opportunity to practice this art and skill. For each situation below, generate effective follow-up questions that would deepen and extend the conversation. We've provided a snippet of conversation for the first example to get you started.

   a. Two classmates who have never met are seated in the classroom before class begins.

      Bob: Hi; my name's Bob. What's yours?
      Sue: Hi; I'm Sue.
      Bob: I've never taken a philosophy course before; have you? What do you think this course will be like?
      Sue: Well, I've never taken a philosophy course either, but I expect there will be lots of reading. And I've heard that the professor's tests are pretty tough.

Bob: Oh great; is it too late to drop?! When you say the tests are tough, tough in what way? Do you mean they cover lots of material, the prof's a hard grader, or what?

b. At a fraternity/sorority mixer, a woman and a man are introduced to each other for the first time by other members of their organizations.

c. After a staff meeting, two new coworkers who will be working on the same important project introduce themselves to each other.

5. As a class, develop a list of categories of information for self-disclosure. For example, categories could include academic achievement, religion, family background, cultural heritage, romantic experiences, and sexuality. Then have each class member write down (privately) something that pertains to each category that the person *would* and *would not* feel comfortable disclosing to another person. For example, under the category of family background, an item that might be disclosed could be that one's parents were divorced; an item that might not be disclosed could be that one suffered emotional or physical abuse in one's family. This activity will help you clarify your own "rules" about self-disclosing personal information.

Chapter 2.1   *Practice Test*

MULTIPLE CHOICE.   Choose the *best* answer to each of the following questions.

1. When asking questions of someone you have just met, you should

    a. limit yourself to yes/no questions.

    b. focus on questions that are personal in nature.

    c. ask questions quickly, moving from one to the next.

    d. tailor the questions to what you have observed about the other.

2. Susan does not feel comfortable communicating with others, but her boyfriend loves socializing. Susan appreciates this about him because he takes "center stage" when they are with people and she can stay in the background. This exemplifies which principle of interpersonal attraction?

    a. proximity

    b. matching hypothesis

    c. similarity

    d. complementarity

3. When you meet someone for the first time, you tend to

    a. reveal your less attractive qualities to the other.

    b. focus on differences between you and the other.

    c. reveal your more attractive qualities to the other.

    d. reveal extremely personal information about yourself to the other.

4. Rick and Ryan were best friends, but since Ryan moved away they have not been as close. Ryan's wife, Kristen, does not understand what the problem is. She tells Ryan that she has had no

problem staying close to her friends since they moved. This difference is because men build closeness through

    a. low disclosure.

    b. high disclosure.

    c. shared activities.

    d. talking.

5. According to Altman and Taylor's social penetration model, intimate relationships are characterized by self-disclosures that are

    a. broad but not deep.

    b. deep but not broad.

    c. broad and deep.

    d. neither broad nor deep.

6. Derek spots an attractive woman at a party and asks his friend whether he knows her. This illustrates what type of uncertainty reduction strategy?

    a. active

    b. passive

    c. interactive

    d. third party

7. One of Jim's first assignments at his new job is to complete a project with his coworker Sally. Sally and Jim work well together during the project, but once it is complete they rarely see each other. The relationship between Jim and Sally is best described as a

    a. relationship of choice.

    b. relationship of attraction.

    c. relationship of circumstance.

    d. relationship of emotion.

8. Walking across campus, seeing other students, and briefly saying "Hi" is an example of

    a. interpersonal communication.

b. self-disclosure.

c. attraction.

d. impersonal communication.

9. Luke will talk with anyone about both his background and his current activities and interests. This information is in Luke's

a. blind area.

b. unknown area.

c. hidden area.

d. open area.

10. Morgan has a crush on Brody. When he is around, she moves to sit closer to him, increases her eye contact, smiles more, and fidgets with her hair. In order to communicate her attraction to Brody, Morgan is using

a. nonverbal immediacy.

b. complimentarity.

c. passive strategies.

d. active strategies.

11. When receiving a compliment, it is best to

a. just say "thank you."

b. agree with the compliment.

c. disagree with the complimenter.

d. try to talk the person out of the compliment.

12. Partners in a "well-minded" relationship will do all of the following *except*

a. ask each other about feelings and behaviors.

b. use head nods and eye contact during conversations.

c. keep head nods and eye contact to a minimum during conversations.

d. be familiar with their partner's opinions and preferences.

13. Physical and sexual attraction

a. are the same thing.

b. are different kinds of appeal.

c. are not influenced by culture.

d. remain fairly constant over time.

14. The direct expression of emotion typically occurs

a. only in the more critical early stages of a relationship.

b. primarily in the middle stages of a relationship.

c. typically at the later stages of a relationship.

d. throughout the entire relationship.

15. If you develop a friendship with someone in one of your classes, more than likely he or she

a. sits fairly far away from you in class.

b. is physically dissimilar to you.

c. sits fairly close to you in class.

d. is not as physically attractive as you are.

16. Brayden has decided to rush a social fraternity. As part of deciding which fraternity he would like to pledge, he attends a number of meetings and parties and watches the way the active members interact. He also listens in on their conversations with one another in the cafeteria. Brayden's uncertainty reduction strategies can best be described as

a. passive.

b. active.

c. reactive.

d. interactive.

17. Manda cannot stand being alone, so she is constantly planning things to do and inviting her friends to join in. Will Schutz might describe Manda as being motivated by her need for

a. inclusion.

b. immediacy.

c. affection.

d. control.

18. Using the same pick-up lines for each new encounter violates which of the principles of effective communication?

    a. Principle 1

    b. Principle 2

    c. Principle 4

    d. Principle 5

19. When Matias told his boss that he felt he had too many projects to work on at once, his boss replied, "I realize you think you have a lot of projects. I have to oversee all of your projects, as well as manage the Darden account, handle annual reviews, and prepare a report to the executive committee. I really know how it is to be overloaded." Matias's boss then explained in detail the stresses of being a leader and manager. The boss effectively demonstrated

    a. empathy.

    b. sympathy.

    c. a self-absorbed communicator style.

    d. appropriate self-disclosure.

20. According to the Johari Window, as relationships progress, we learn about ourselves from our relational partners because they tell us things they know about us that we did not know. As this happens, the _____ quadrant shrinks and the _____ expands.

    a. blind; open

    b. hidden; open

    c. unknown; open

    d. open; unknown

TRUE/FALSE. Indicate whether the following statements are *true* or *false*.

1. T or F   In general, we are attracted to people who are similar to us.

2. T or F   A person who continually talks about himself is termed a conversational narcissist.

3. T or F   A family relationship begins as a relationship of choice.

4. T or F   Relational partners typically seek a balance between the potential risks and rewards of self-disclosure.

5. T or F   Men tend to describe their relationships as less satisfying because they form out of sharing activities instead of sharing communication.

6. T or F   Interactive strategies for uncertainty reduction are those that are conducted online.

7. T or F   A majority of people report flirting the same way whether online or face to face.

8. T or F   Relationships with family members are considered relationships of circumstance.

9. T or F   Impersonal communication involves mutual influence and treating one another as unique.

10. T or F   Sexual attraction is the degree to which we find another person physically appealing.

FILL IN THE BLANK. Complete the following statements.

1. Communicating directly with someone to try to learn something about him or her is an example of a(n) _____ strategy for reducing uncertainty.

2. A relationship that you intentionally seek out and develop is a relationship of _____.

3. _____ communication occurs between two people who simultaneously attempt to mutually influence each other.

4. _____ is voluntarily providing other people with information about yourself that they would not know otherwise.

5. Lisa and Dedra first met at the grocery store when they both rounded a corner at the same

time and crashed their carts into each other. This is an example of a relationship of _____.

6. The extent to which you want to begin or maintain a relationship with someone is a measure of your interpersonal _____ to that person.

7. _____ theory argues that you are driven to increase the predictability of interpersonal circumstances.

8. Watching someone else to try to learn something about him or her is an example of a(n) _____ strategy for reducing uncertainty.

9. If a salesclerk communicates with all of his or her customers as if they were objects and not individuals, he or she is practicing _____ communication.

10. The _____ hypothesis suggests that you will tend to seek out people who are as physically attractive as you are.

Enhancing Relationships

CHAPTER OBJECTIVES

After studying this chapter, you should be able to

1. Explain how the five communication principles for a lifetime apply to interpersonal communication among friends, family members, and coworkers.

2. Identify the interpersonal communication skills that are most critical for effectiveness in the workplace.

3. Identify and describe the five stages of relational escalation.

4. Identify and describe the five stages of relational de-escalation.

5. Define interpersonal conflict and distinguish between constructive and destructive conflict.

6. Discuss power dynamics in complementary, symmetrical, and parallel interpersonal relationships.

7. Explain the difference between assertive and aggressive communication.

8. Explain the key characteristics of nonconfrontational, confrontational, and cooperative styles of conflict management.

9. Discuss the major ways to manage emotions, information, goals, and problems in conflict situations.

Relationship is a pervading and changing mystery . . . brutal or lovely, the mystery waits for people wherever they go, whatever extreme they run to.

Eudora Welty

Pal Szinyel Merse, Picnic in May. © SuperStock, Inc.

W hat makes you happy in this life? Think a bit before answering that question. What really gives you enjoyment? Staring at a computer screen? Working on a project for your job? Reading a great book? Playing a video game? Being by yourself, writing in your journal? Taking a long walk? Let us venture a guess: While any one of these things might bring some level of pleasure into your life, none of them could be considered *the* thing in life that gives you the most enjoyment. Probably most of us would answer that question with some response that involves other people or, perhaps, only one other person. Our family members, friends, and coworkers are very important to us.

To some degree, we all come from dysfunctional families—there is no such thing as a perfect, or "functional," family. As Tolstoy said, "Happy families are all alike; every unhappy family is unhappy in its own way." But no matter how imperfect our families are, no matter how crazy our siblings used to make us (or still make us), or how far apart we feel we may have grown from family members, almost all of us would agree that family relationships are extremely important. Likewise, when people talk about their jobs and what they like best about where they work, most often they talk about the people they work with. So, disregarding the few true hermits out there, most of us are "people who need people." It may sound corny, but we all know that our relationships with other people are what bring us joy.

In Chapter 2.1 we examined some fundamental aspects of interpersonal communication that facilitate online and face-to-face relationships. We discussed attraction and those first conversations that can launch relationships or stop them dead in their tracks. In this chapter we move forward to discuss interpersonal communication as it occurs in ongoing relationships. Where appropriate, we describe how interpersonal communication functions to maintain and, in some situations, terminate online relationships, but our primary focus in this chapter is the good old-fashioned, face-to-face relationship. We attempt to answer the question, Once a relationship has been initiated, how does it progress?

First, let's reconsider our five communication principles for a lifetime as they pertain to certain relationships. Most of our examples in this chapter and the previous one tend to focus on romantic relationships, so we want to explore in some detail how communication principles apply to three other types of relationships most people experience: friendships, family relationships, and relationships with colleagues.

Aware
Verbal
Nonverbal
Listen and Respond
Adapt

The Importance of Friendship

One of the best definitions of a friend, attributed to Aristotle, is "a soul that resides in two bodies." A friend is someone we like and who likes us. We trust our friends and share good and bad times with them. We enjoy being with them, so we try to make time for that purpose. We expect a certain level of self-sacrifice from our friends. For example, you know you've got a good friend when that person gives up something (like a hot date) just to help you through a tough time.

Researchers have examined some differences among friendships at four stages in life: childhood, adolescence, adulthood, and old age.[1] When we start to talk (around the age of two), we begin to play and interact with others and perceive playmates as those who can help meet our needs. Our first friendships are typically superficial, self-centered, and fleeting, because they are based on momentary sharing of activities.[2] As we grow, we develop more of a give-and-take in friendships. During adolescence we move away from relationships with parents and toward greater intimacy with our peers. At this point in our development, peer relationships are the most important social influence on our behavior. Adolescents are likely to join groups, such as a sports or debate team, or, unfortunately, less socially desirable groups bent on violence and destruction of property.

Adult friendships are among our most valued relationships, even though they may be few in number. Research has found that, on average, adults have ten to twenty casual friends, four to six close friends, and only one to two best friends.[3] Rather than progressing through a series of stages in which intimacy deepens, which is typical of romantic relationships, friendships often alternate between periods of development and deterioration.[4]

As Americans continue to spend more hours at work each year, we often find that our closest friends are also our coworkers.[5] We share common interests, concerns, and schedules with coworkers, so it's natural for colleagues to fulfill each others' social needs as well. No doubt some of you reading this text are working a job, taking classes that demand significant blocks of time, and juggling all of this with a home and family life. Given all this activity, you may find that friendships get less of your attention. Unless we make maintaining friendships a priority, we may find ourselves becoming too busy to "work them in" and, sadly, losing them over time.

A new term has emerged for what we suspect is a long-standing phenomenon: "friends with benefits." Sexual liaisons between persons who are supposed to be "just friends" have been popularized through such television shows as *Sex and the City, Jake in Progress,* and a *Seinfeld* episode entitled "The Deal." Such media exposure has spurred research into this unique form of relationship. Communication scholars Mikayla Hughes, Kelly Morrison, and Kelli Jean Asada define the "friends with benefits" relationship (FWBR) as one that emerges from a pre-existing friendship but that evolves to include sexual activity. The sexual contact does not change the friendship into a romantic relationship or imply a commitment; in fact, the people involved in an FWBR do not want anything more from their partners than what they have. These researchers explain that "these types of relationships are distinct in that they combine both the benefits of friendship with the benefits of a sexual relationship, yet avoid the responsibilities and commitment that romantic sexual relationships typically entail."[6]

The FWBR differs from a "hookup"—a casual one-night sexual encounter that has also been observed among college student populations—in that it is

Many people find that the friendships they maintain over the years are among their most valuable.

more long-lasting and stable because it builds on a pre-existing friendship.[7] Hughes and her colleagues discovered that FWBRs are relatively common on college campuses today, that participants in such relationships perceive them as important, and that the relationships function effectively, provided both participants adhere to the following rules.

1. FWBR participants must maintain their original friendship, meaning that sexual activity doesn't change the friendship and the participants continue to do things together that they typically did as friends.
2. Emotions don't become involved, or the FWBR will be at risk.
3. The FWBR is maintained in secret, even if, for some people, this means that their romantic/sexual partners don't know about the FWBR.
4. The relationship may be renegotiated, with either participant opting out at any time.[8]

We don't know your views about this kind of relationship, whether your moral or religious views preclude your acceptance of the FWBR as a viable relational form, or whether you've had or currently have this type of relationship in your life, but it is an interesting type of relationship that communication researchers have begun to study.

Friendships are extremely important in old age.[9] During retirement, when many individuals have more time for socializing, friendships become increasingly critical. Older adults tend to rely on enduring friendships and to maintain a small, highly valued network of friends.

Communication Principles for a Lifetime: Enhancing Friendships

Noted author and motivational speaker Dale Carnegie suggested, "You can make more friends in two months by becoming interested in other people than you can in two years by trying to get other people interested in you."[10] Attraction is what draws you to potential friends, just as various forms of attraction draw you to potential dates or romantic partners. So how do you reveal your interpersonal attraction to someone so as to form a friendship?

Like many other things, friendship development begins with an awareness of yourself—Principle One. Knowing your own interests, likes, and dislikes is a first step if you are trying to expand your circle of friends. If, for example, you consider yourself a spiritual person, then you're more likely to make new friends with those kinds of people at a church gathering or in a yoga and meditation class than in some other setting.

Aware

We need communication to initiate, develop, deepen, and maintain friendships. Principles Two and Three, which involve the effective use of verbal and nonverbal communication, are essential in friendship. Our verbal communication tends to become more frequent and to deepen as friendships develop. We also use immediacy cues to establish friendships—behaviors that reveal our liking of other people, such as leaning forward, moving closer, making eye contact, smiling, and nodding in response to others.

Verbal
Nonverbal

Listening and responding are important communication skills in friendship. Most of us don't stay friends with people who don't seem to listen to us, or who listen but respond inappropriately. With friends, it's important to be aware of what they *say* as well as what they *do,* as we attempt to read what's going on with them and determine the best response. That may be an empathic response that allows your friend to vent or emote while you merely attempt to feel what your friend is feeling. Your best response on other occasions may be to offer advice and counsel. Probably no other communication skill develops a friendship more than the ability to listen and respond appropriately.

Listen and Respond

QUICK REVIEW

Finally, we learn to adapt to our friends or they probably don't stay our friends for very long (Principle Five). This means that we extend different parts of ourselves and communicate differently with various friends. You may enjoy your dancing buddies because you can let a creative, wilder side of yourself show with them, while you communicate more seriously as you study with a group of classmates who have become your friends.

Adapt

The Importance of Family

Of all the relationships we experience in our lifetimes, none are more complicated than family relationships. Family members have the power to shape our self-concepts and affect self-esteem more than other people. Granted, at some point we can choose to stop or lessen the effect family members can have on our

lives. But for most of us, those early messages we received as children, primarily from our parents and secondarily from our siblings, still remain in our psyches and affect who we are today.

To say that family life has changed is an understatement. Family units are dramatically different than they were when the predominant profile was a two-parent, father-as-bread-winner, mother-as-homemaker arrangement.[11] In the 1980s, the New York Supreme Court provided a very broad definition of a family, stating that "The best description of a family is a continuing relationship of love and care, and an assumption of responsibility for some other person."[12] Estimates for the first part of the new century suggest that the most common profile of American family is the step-family, or blended family.[13]

Communication Principles for a Lifetime: Enhancing Family Relationships

Aware

Growing up in families, we begin to discover who we are and how we should communicate with others. If you were raised by the rule of "children should be seen and not heard," then you got clear messages about when it was appropriate to speak out and when to be silent. If you witnessed a good deal of conflict in your family, you no doubt have been affected by that experience. You may have turned out to be someone who avoids conflict at all costs, but research suggests that it is more likely that you will engage in the same form of conflict you witnessed or participated in as you grew up.[14] In addition, research shows that family interaction patterns affect people's views of their own communication abilities.[15] People who grow up in a *pluralistic* family environment—one that is highly conversational and that encourages children to develop and express opinions about the world without fear of rejection or negative consequences from their parents—tend to perceive themselves as being skilled communicators in their friendships and romantic relationships. Those who grow up in families that encourage conformity and that do not expose children to other ways of thinking or controversial views of the world tend to believe less in their own abilities to communicate effectively in relationships, particularly when it comes to self-disclosing to others.

Our earliest lessons about verbal and nonverbal communication come from our families. Virginia Satir has conducted extensive research on family communication.[16] She suggests that in healthy families, "the members' sense of self-worth is high; communication is direct, clear, specific, and honest; rules are flexible, humane, and subject to change; and the family's links to society are open and hopeful." In such families, Satir notes, people listen actively; they look *at* one another, not *through* one another or at the floor; they treat children as people; they touch one another affectionately regardless of age; and they openly discuss disappointments, fears, hurts, angers, and criticism, as well as joys and achievements. The degree to which parents and children can reveal what they are thinking and feeling is a measure of family cohesiveness. Another aspect Satir highlights corresponds to our Principle Four, that of listening and responding. Healthy family relationships are built on foundations of trust, which involves listening to one another and responding helpfully. Many conflicts arise because family members don't listen well to one another and respond based on that faulty listening.

Verbal
Nonverbal

Listen and Respond

Finally, family relationships involve a good deal of adaptation, particularly when, as adults, we visit our parents. Here's an example: A colleague of ours describes the tension he feels when he visits his parents on certain holidays. His father was born in 1920, so he has very different experiences and values than his 40-something son. During key moments (like over Thanksgiving dinner), when the father begins to talk in stereotypes (usually derogatory) about certain racial or ethnic groups, the son cringes. He must decide whether to engage his dad and risk ruining the occasion for his mother (which he has done at times) or squelch his own views, which could be seen as an act of cowardice and a tacit acceptance of racism. Most of the time now he says he "keeps the peace," adapting his communication for the higher goal of avoiding conflict and keeping the family holiday pleasant.

WATCH

QUICK
REVIEW

Adapt

The Importance of Colleagues

For many of us, our work is our livelihood, our most time-consuming activity. In fact, many Americans are working longer hours—10% more time on the job in the twenty-first century than 30 years ago.[17] Many things make a job worthwhile and rewarding, but most working people say that relationships with people they work with make the most difference between job satisfaction and dissatisfaction.

What are the most important skills people need to be successful on the job? Year after year, the number-one skill employers look for in new hires is the ability to communicate effectively with others.[18] You land your job through a face-to-face interview (in most cases). You keep your job based on your ability to do the work and get along with coworkers and bosses, which usually involves a large amount of interpersonal interaction.

The best managers listen carefully and then respond effectively.

Communication Principles for a Lifetime: Enhancing Workplace Relationships

Getting accustomed to a new job takes a while. There are the rudimentary things to discover and adjust to, such as finding out where to park or which subway or bus route to take, learning the procedures that make an organization function, and observing general office protocol. Then there are the more important things, like learning how to do your job well, ascertaining the chain of command, and discovering which colleagues have the potential to develop into friends.

When most of us enter a new situation, such as a new job, we experience uncertainty. We discussed in Chapter 2.1 how the motivation to reduce uncertainty causes us to seek information. On the job, our uncertainty will most likely be reduced by those who hired us, those who are assigned to train or orient us to the new situation, and coworkers who are at our same level within the organization. We are most likely to use passive strategies first, meaning that we observe our surroundings and how people interact on the job, as a way of becoming more aware so that we will know how to behave appropriately (Principle One). Perception checking with colleagues also increases awareness. For example, after attending your first staff meeting, you might want to ask a few colleagues whether the gathering was typical of the kind of staff meetings the organization holds.

As we begin to interact with persons of varying status in the organization, we draw on our most effective verbal and nonverbal communication skills so that we make positive impressions on others (Principles Two and Three). The higher you go in an organization, the more your job involves communicating with others. In one research project, scholar Harvey Mintzberg observed chief executive officers for five weeks. He found that managers spend almost 80% of their day communicating orally with others.[19] In most organizations, working is communication; communicating is working.

One skill that makes for an effective worker—any worker, in any organization—is the ability to listen and respond effectively to colleagues (Principle Four). The best managers of other people are the best listeners. They listen patiently, fully, and nonjudgmentally. They also exercise caution before responding, so that they will respond appropriately.

Finally, our Principle Five about adaptation is critical to successful coworker relationships. You cannot hope to be successful on the job if you com-

Aware

Verbal
Nonverbal

Listen and Respond

municate the same way to your boss as you do to your peers on the job, your subordinates, and others in your life—including long-term friends, intimates, and family members. This may seem obvious, but we find that people sometimes experience isolation on the job because they cannot get along with coworkers. Or they've trusted coworkers too much and revealed personal information, only to have that information used against them later. Some people don't realize that they can't talk at work about everything they talk about at home. They don't adapt to the situation, and it often costs them their jobs.

Adapt

QUICK REVIEW

Stages of Relationship Development

Researchers have determined that relationships develop in discernible stages, although they differ in their use of terms and the number of stages.[20] While the research on relational stages is most often applied to dating or romantic relationships, the information can also apply to other types of relationships.

Verbal Nonverbal

    Understanding these stages is important. First, interpersonal communication is affected by the stage of the relationship. For instance, individuals in an advanced stage discuss topics and display nonverbal behaviors that rarely appear in the early stages of a relationship. Second, interpersonal communication facilitates movement between the various stages. Relationships change and are continually renegotiated by those involved. Interpersonal communication moves a relationship forward as we progress from being acquaintances, to friends, to lovers, and, possibly, to marital or committed partners. Ideally, communication should move a relationship back from partners to friends as well, although regressing a relationship is difficult to accomplish. Research indicates that after a breakup, couples who continue to have something of value to offer to each other, such as status or information, are likely to maintain a friendship. But former romantic couples who experience barriers to friendship, such as negative reactions by friends and family or the development of a new romantic relationship, are unlikely to be able to become friends.[21]

    It's helpful to think of relational stages as floors in a high rise (see Figure 2.2.1). The bottom floor represents a first meeting; the penthouse is intimacy. Relational development is an elevator that stops at every floor. As you ascend, you might get off the elevator and wander around for a while before going to the next floor. Each time you get on, you don't know how many floors up the elevator will take you or how long you will stay at any given floor. In fact, sometimes you never get back on the elevator, electing instead to stay at a particular stage of relational development. This may represent stability or stagnation. Stability is not the same as stagnation; it may simply mean that a relationship has reached a comfortable point for both partners. But notice that we say *both* partners; if one partner feels the relationship has stabilized at an appropriate stage, but the other partner feels the relationship has stagnated, dissatisfaction and conflict are often the result.

FIGURE 2.2.1

Relationship Stages

Source: From Steven A. Beebe, Susan J. Beebe, and Mark V. Redmond, *Interpersonal Communication: Relating to Others*, 3/e. Published by Allyn and Bacon, Boston, MA. Copyright © 2002 by Pearson Education. Reprinted by permission of the publisher.

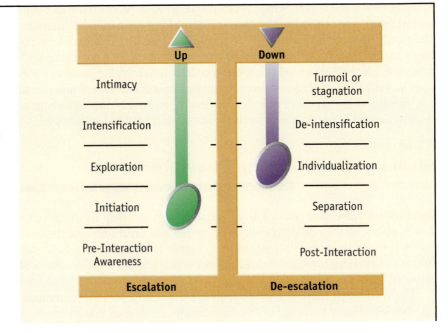

If you fall head over heels in love, you might want to escalate quickly from floor to floor toward intimacy, possibly even skipping some floors. The process of de-escalating a relationship does not occur in every relationship, but if it does, it may be a slow or quick descent through various floors. The best approach to relationship development is to share this elevator with your partner, so that the two of you make decisions about how high you will ride the elevator, how long to stay at each floor, and whether to take the elevator back down. Often partners do not share decisions about movement within the relationship. Sometimes one of the partners rides the elevator alone. Let's explore in more depth this process of escalating and de-escalating relationships.

Relational Escalation

As depicted in Figure 2.2.1, the first level of relational development is termed **the pre-interaction awareness stage. In this stage, you might observe a person or even talk with others about that person without having any direct interaction.** You might not move beyond the pre-interaction awareness stage if your impressions of the person aren't favorable or the circumstances aren't right.

If you are attracted to the other person and the circumstances are right, you might proceed to **the initiation stage. First conversations typically involve each person responding to the other's questions as they try to determine what they have in common.** Try to ask engaging questions and

Aware

VISUAL LITERACY

At the intensification stage, a couple's relationship becomes the central focus of their lives.

then listen carefully to the answers. The answers suggest follow-up questions that can draw the person out and make you both more comfortable. Your nonverbal behavior should also indicate your interest.

If you decide to go to **the exploration stage, you will begin to share more in-depth information.** You will probably have minimal physical contact and you may limit the amount of time you spend together because you are building a relationship. But it's important to realize that some relationships move through stages very quickly. For example, we probably all know people whose relationships were extremely physical, and perhaps sexual, from the very start. Are those relationships doomed because they didn't follow set or prescribed paths for development? No; some relationships may just proceed through stages faster than others. However, relationships that are extremely physical or sexual may burn out quickly because they lack the emotional foundation necessary to survive.

If you proceed to **the intensification stage, you will start to depend on each other for self-confirmation, meaning that your partner's opinion of or feelings about you weigh more heavily than those of others. Partners tend to spend more time together, increase the variety of activities they share, adopt more intimate physical distance and contact, and personalize their language.** The frequency and level of shared personal information increases and deepens, and the couple may decide to label their connection.

The top level of relationship escalation is **the intimacy stage. Partners who are in this stage provide primary confirmation of each other's**

Verbal
Nonverbal
Listen and Respond

self-concept, meaning that your partner knows how you view your-self and accepts that view. Communication is highly personalized and synchronized. Partners talk about anything and everything, and a commitment to maintaining the relationship might even be formalized and socially recognized, such as with a decision to marry. The partners share an understanding of each other's language and nonverbal cues and have a great deal of physical contact. They use fewer words to communicate effectively because they understand each other without words. Reaching this stage takes time—time to build trust, share personal information, observe each other in various situations, and create an emotional bond and commitment.

RECAP

Relational Escalation

Stage	Explanation
Pre-Interaction Awareness	You become aware of your attraction to someone and begin to observe that person.
Initiation	You initiate contact with the person with whom you want a relationship.
Exploration	Interactions deepen as questions and answers elicit more information from partners.
Intensification	Partners begin to depend on each other for confirmation of their self-concepts. They spend more time together, engage in more intimate touch, and personalize their language.
Intimacy	Partners provide primary confirmation of each other's self-concept. Verbally, language is highly personalized; nonverbal behaviors are synchronized.

Relational De-Escalation

Sometimes relationships begin to unravel; this can happen for a variety of reasons. Some unravel to the point of termination. But as you may already know, ending a relationship is not as simple as going down the same way you came up; it is not a mere reversal of the escalation process.[22]

Communication scholar Mark Knapp provides a model for how relationships come apart.[23] When an intimate relationship is not going well, it usually enters a stage of either turmoil or stagnation. The turmoil stage involves an increase in conflict, as one or both partners find more faults in the other. The definition of the relationship seems to lose its clarity, and

Ethics and *Communication*

Making Breaking Up Easier to Do?

Students in an interpersonal communication class were discussing online relationships, when one said a surprising thing: "I got a break-up notice over the Internet once. I couldn't believe it; this girl actually had the nerve to break up with me through an e-mail message. We never ever discussed it face-to-face or over the phone." No one in the class had heard of a "Dear John" message being conveyed online.

Breakups are tough, but what is a person's ethical obligation when she or he wishes to terminate a relationship? The Internet allows for a certain level of impersonality, but is sending an e-mail an appropriate way to "dump" someone? Would you want someone to break up with you in such a "high-tech" way?

mutual acceptance declines. **The communication climate is tense; interactions are difficult and forced. Stagnation occurs when the relationship loses its vitality and the partners become complacent, taking each other for granted. Communication and physical contact between the partners decrease; they spend less time together but don't necessarily engage in conflict.** Partners in a stagnating relationship tend to go through the motions of an intimate relationship without the commitment or the joy; they simply follow their established relational routines. But a stagnating relationship can be salvaged. A relationship can remain in turmoil or stagnate for a long time, but the individuals can repair, redefine, or revitalize the relationship and return to intimacy.

If the turmoil or stagnation continues, however, the individuals will likely experience **the de-intensification stage. This involves significantly decreased interaction; increased physical, emotional, and psychological distance; and decreased dependence on the other for self-confirmation.** The partners might discuss the definition of their relationship, question its future, and assess each other's level of dissatisfaction. The relationship can be repaired and the individuals can move once again toward intensification and intimacy, but it's more difficult to accomplish at this point.

VISUAL
LITERACY

After de-intensification, **the individualization stage occurs. Partners tend to define their lives more as individuals and less as a couple or unit.** Neither views the other as a partner or significant other any more. Interactions are limited, and the perspective changes from "we" and "us" to "you" and "me." Both partners tend to turn to others for confirmation of their self-concepts; physical intimacy is at an all-time low, if not nonexistent; and nonverbal distance is easily detected.

In the separation stage, individuals make an intentional decision to minimize or eliminate further interpersonal interaction. If they share custody of children, attend mutual family gatherings, or work at the same place, the nature of their interactions changes. They divide property, resources, and friends. Early interactions in this stage are often tense and difficult, especially if the relationship has been intimate.

Although interaction may cease, the effect of a relationship is not over. Relationships—even failed ones—are powerful experiences in our lives. The final level in relational de-escalation is termed **the post-interaction stage. This level represents the lasting effects the relationship has on the self, and therefore on other interactions and relationships.** Relationship scholar Steve Duck explains that in this final stage of terminating relationships, we engage in "grave-dressing"—we create a public statement for people who ask why we broke up or why we're no longer friends with someone. It also means that we come to grips with losing the relationship.[24] Sometimes our sense of self gets battered during the final stages of a relationship; we have to work hard to regain a healthy sense of self.

Prepare yourself for some news, if you haven't already heard this: In February 2004, just before Valentine's Day, Barbie and Ken officially broke up. Having met on the set of a television commercial in 1961, the two had been inseparable ever since . . . until now. A spokesperson for Mattel said that Barbie and Ken felt it was "time to spend some quality time apart"; however, the two say that they will remain friends. Apparently even dolls can experience the heartbreak of termination of a relationship.[25]

Research over several decades has shed light on how people prefer to end relationships, as well as how they prefer someone to end a relationship with them.[26] In most relationships, the breakup is unilateral (done by one party) rather than bilateral (agreed to by both parties). Studies show that most people use and prefer indirect breakup strategies, such as avoidance, requests for "distance" or "space" in the relationship, a general fading away rather than an abrupt or definite breakup, and the staging of a conflict that leads to blaming and relationship termination. Direct breakup strategies, typically accomplished face to face, are probably the most interpersonally communicative but not the most preferred by most people in relationships. Being told we're being dumped just isn't something too many of us prefer to experience. If you're really sheepish about breaking up with someone and you have some money to burn, a payment of $50 to the Web site breakupservice.com will buy you the services of someone who will call or write a letter and break up your relationship for you. An employee of the service will even pick up any possessions you've left in the care of your ex and make sure they get returned to you. The service's employees report a significant increase in business just after major holidays.

What typifies each of the different relational stages of escalation and de-escalation is the communication—verbal and nonverbal—that is present or absent. Interpersonal communication facilitates movement through the stages of escalation; the lack of communication moves people through the stages of de-escalation.

Technology *and* Communication

Cheating in Cyberspace

Research reveals that the primary use for the home computer is relationship maintenance, mainly in the form of e-mailing to keep in touch with family members and friends.[27] Another, less mainstream, use of the personal computer is to establish "liaisons" outside one's primary relationship. Typically, these liaisons don't begin as sexual relationships. They may begin through common interests, such as those you may share with someone who posts frequently in a chat room, for example; after a while you decide to begin exchanging comments with only that person in a private chat room. Since these exchanges are anonymous (chatters most often use pseudonyms), a private exchange between two chatters seems harmless, but this form of cyber-relationship can escalate and take on another level of intimacy and meaning.

We've probably all heard of cybersex—sexual activity that occurs online, but without any physical contact between participants—but you may not have thought about the damage cybersex can do to a monogamous, committed relationship. Most people have negative reactions to marital infidelity, whether they themselves have experienced it or know someone who has; even those who haven't experienced it say that they would respond negatively to a partner's infidelity if it were to happen.[28] But few people in committed, monogamous relationships think much about cyber-infidelity—until it happens to them. Is online cheating really *cheating* in the traditional sense? No physical contact has taken place; the sexual activity is accomplished through verbal exchanges within virtual reality—so how real is virtual reality? Should cyber-infidelity affect a committed relationship as much as in-person infidelity, or is it somehow different?

Putting a positive spin on this situation, some research suggests that people who form sexual liaisons online are able to explore their sexuality with little concern that friends, coworkers, and spouses will discover their activities.[29] People may feel sexually hindered in their face-to-face relationships, so in a sense, the Internet becomes the arena in which their "true" sexual selves find expression. They may come to understand themselves better sexually because they feel under less pressure, and the benefits of such discovery can carry over into their face-to-face relationships. Some are drawn to the Internet for sexual gratification if their in-person relationships are in turmoil or decline and their opportunities for sexual expression and gratification are limited. In addition, since online sexual exchanges don't occur in person, the eroticism is based on other factors, such as emotional intimacy and verbal expressiveness, rather than on physical attractiveness. Concerns about STDs or unwanted pregnancies disappear. A final benefit cited in research relates to the fact that if a virtual sexual liaison goes awry, participants don't suffer such consequences as in-person retribution or confrontation, since online exchanges, for the most part, remain anonymous, with true identities withheld.

One study asked participants about their online sexual activity, including what initially motivated them to engage in cybersex, why they continued to engage in it, the role it played in their lives, and the effects it had on them.[30] Interestingly enough, 41% of subjects revealed that they did not believe that online sexual activity constituted cheating on a partner under any circumstances. Fourteen percent believed it to be cheating if a person engaged in cybersex repeatedly with the same person. Smaller percentages of participants believed that online sex was cheating only if interactive video cameras were used or if the online sex led to phone sex. Thirty-three percent of subjects believed that online sex was cheating and that it was just as much an act of infidelity as in-person sex with someone other than one's partner.

What's your view of cybersex? Should someone who is in a monogamous, committed, face-to-face relationship be seeking sexual liaisons over the Internet? Does online sexual activity constitute a breach of faith with one's partner, or is it merely an exercise in "sexploration" that has no bearing on one's primary relationship?

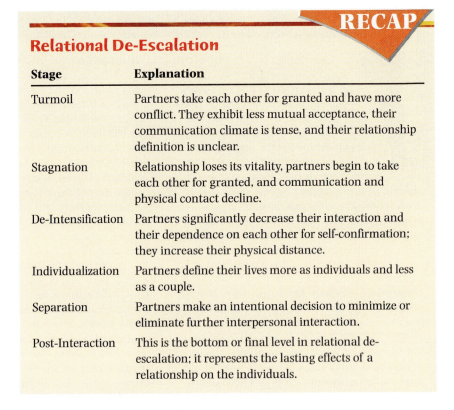

RECAP

Relational De-Escalation

Stage	Explanation
Turmoil	Partners take each other for granted and have more conflict. They exhibit less mutual acceptance, their communication climate is tense, and their relationship definition is unclear.
Stagnation	Relationship loses its vitality, partners begin to take each other for granted, and communication and physical contact decline.
De-Intensification	Partners significantly decrease their interaction and their dependence on each other for self-confirmation; they increase their physical distance.
Individualization	Partners define their lives more as individuals and less as a couple.
Separation	Partners make an intentional decision to minimize or eliminate further interpersonal interaction.
Post-Interaction	This is the bottom or final level in relational de-escalation; it represents the lasting effects of a relationship on the individuals.

Managing Interpersonal Conflict

A World of Conflict

We live in a world full of conflict. You can hardly watch the news on television, listen to a radio talk show, or read a newspaper headline without being confronted with another story of conflict. Whether it's the Middle East, a political coup in a country in Africa, or a disturbance generated by extremist groups right here at home, conflict on a global scale seems inevitable. While conflicts throughout the world have always existed, the events of September 11, 2001, launched the United States into a series of intense conflicts across the globe. How can we understand conflict on such a scale? What can we learn about conflict that might help mediate its destructive effect across the world? An understanding of conflict and the development of effective communication skills to manage conflict begins one-on-one, in our day-to-day relationships. Conflict is rooted in interpersonal communication.

Do you know the three most important words a person can say to someone? The answer isn't "I love you"; the answer is "I was wrong." These words are actually better to hear than "I'm sorry," because saying you're sorry could mean that you're sorry you're having a disagreement or you're sorry you got caught doing something that caused the conflict, or it could be just something to say in an attempt to end the conflict. It's quite hard for most of us to admit that we were at fault, but it's very meaningful in a conflict situation when someone admits that she or he was wrong.

Interpersonal conflict is a struggle that occurs when two people cannot agree on a way to meet their needs. When needs are incompatible, if there are too few resources to satisfy them, or if individuals opt to compete rather than to cooperate to satisfy them, then conflict occurs. The intensity of a conflict usually relates to the intensity of the unmet needs. The bedrock of all conflict is differences—different goals, experiences, expectations, and so forth.

Humans are generally need driven and goal oriented, so it's not surprising that most conflict is goal driven. You want something; your partner wants something else. If your partner interferes with your achievement of your goal, there may be a conflict. Suppose you are trying to find a place to park in an over-crowded lot on campus. Just as you find an empty spot, another student zips into "your" space. Your blood boils and you get out of your car fighting mad. Or suppose you have had a difficult day at work or school (or both). All you want to do is hunker down with a bowl of popcorn and watch a game (*any* game). But your roommate announces that some mutual friends are coming over for dinner. "That's not what *I* feel like doing tonight. Why didn't you ask *me* before you invited them?" you shout. In both instances, your goals collide head-on with someone else's, and you feel as if you have lost control of the situation.

How Conflict Functions in Relationships

Conflict is a normal, inevitable element within relationships. The more important the relationship, the greater the potential for conflict, because we aren't as likely to voice disagreement with people who don't matter very much to us. Psychologist Phillip McGraw (better known as Dr. Phil) contends that there is a third inevitability in life beyond death and taxes—conflict (or as he terms it, verbal fighting with the one you love).[31] McGraw describes three "fundamental truths" about fighting: (1) Fighting is unquestionably painful; (2) fighting is an unavoidable part of every relationship; and (3) there are right and wrong ways to fight— you just have to learn to conduct disagreements in ways that enhance your relationship.

It's surprising (and disconcerting) when people in relationships say, "We just get along so well; we belong together because we've never even had a fight." While we don't advocate staging or picking a fight with a partner as an experiment, we do believe that it is worrisome to commit to a person when you don't know how she or he handles conflict. If your partner or close friend is a "screamer" and you prefer to walk away from a conflict in silent protest, your relationship is headed for very rough waters. People's responses to conflict must be known quantities if a relationship is to be successful.

HOMEWORK

Conflict Can Be Constructive or Destructive   To construct something is to build or make something new. **Characterized by cooperation in dealing with differences, constructive conflict can help identify which elements of a relationship need to change or be improved, so that new patterns are established.** Here's an example:

Mike: You know, I'm getting tired of always going to your mother's on Sundays. It's like we're in a rut or something. Just one weekend, I'd like to have a Sunday with no schedule or agenda.

Claire: Mike, I thought you liked going over there, because my mom's such a good cook and you and dad are working on that project together. Plus, it's one of the few times I get to spend time with my folks.

Mike: Well, I do like going over there, but not every weekend.

Claire: I didn't realize that you were starting to resent it or feel like you were getting into a rut. Let's talk more about this, and figure something out.

Adapt

Note that Claire recognizes the need for further dialogue about Mike's complaint. She transforms the issue of disagreement into a topic for discussion and relational adjustment. If Mike hadn't expressed his dissatisfaction, the issue might have taken on larger proportions. He might have expressed his feelings of being in a rut in a cruder, more hurtful way on the next drive over to the parents' house, for example. Many times these expressions contain more venom than we intend or actually feel. A well-managed disagreement that includes expressing one's own needs or revising goals can lead couples or friends first to examine and then to revitalize their relationship. Constructive conflict enables both people to view a disagreement from different perspectives, even if the information shared seems negative at first.

A rapidly spiraling **destructive conflict (one that is characterized by a lack of cooperation in dealing with differences and that dismantles relationships without restoring them)** can do as much damage as a tornado churning through a trailer park. A conflict may start over a seemingly small issue, but it increases in intensity as other issues and differences are brought into the discussion. Such destructive escalation blocks off options for managing differences and makes a win–win solution more elusive. The hallmark of destructive conflict is a lack of flexibility in responding to others.[32] Combatants view their differences from a win–lose perspective, rather than looking for solutions that allow each individual to gain. If both individuals are dissatisfied with the outcome of the conflict, then it has been more destructive than constructive.

Listen and Respond

In their book on interpersonal conflict, William Wilmot and Joyce Hocker discuss six hallmarks of constructive conflict, which involve analysis, adaptation, and effective interpersonal communication.[33]

1. *People change.*   In relationships, people are involved with each other. In conflict, people must work hard to stay involved with each other, because an interaction that escalates into conflict can pull people apart. Flexibility and a willingness to change are key. Wilmot and Hocker explain that "rigid, insistent communication defeats the purpose of constructive conflict."

Diversity *and* Communication

Conflict and Culture

*I*nterpersonal conflict is difficult to manage, but cross-cultural conflict can be even more overwhelming. Some people are trained in negotiation and mediation techniques, so that they can facilitate peaceful relations between nations and peoples. But what if you're not planning on becoming an international negotiator? What if you simply want to know a few things to keep you from being tossed in jail in a foreign country?

Intercultural communication scholar Stella Ting-Toomey has written extensively on this subject and produced some insightful information that can help you anticipate and avoid intercultural conflict.[34] Persons from individualistic cultures, such as the United States, emphasize the importance of the individual over the group. Those in collectivistic cultures, such as the

Japanese, emphasize group rather than individual achievement. These differing values contribute to intercultural conflict.

So what should members of individualistic cultures (such as Americans) know when interacting with members of collectivistic cultures? Note the seven assumptions about conflict that individualistic cultures hold; compare this list with the seven assumptions about conflict that collectivistic cultures hold. Then assess the differences.

Not only do members of different cultural groups have different views of conflict, they have vastly different ways of dealing with or managing conflict. It's wise to do some research on the country you will be visiting or moving to, so that you understand how basic cultural values differ from those of your home country.

Individualistic Cultures	Collectivistic Cultures
1. The purpose of conflict is to air out major differences and problems.	1. Conflict is damaging to self-respect and relational harmony; it should be avoided as much as possible.
2. Conflict can be either functional or dysfunctional.	2. For the most part, conflict is dysfunctional.
3. Repressed, unconfronted problems can lead to dysfunctional conflict.	3. Conflict signals a lack of self-discipline and emotional immaturity.
4. Functional conflict provides an opportunity for solving problems.	4. Conflict provides a testing ground for skillful negotiation and "face-saving."
5. Substantive and relational issues in conflict should be handled separately.	5. Substantive and relational issues are always intertwined.
6. Conflict should be handled directly and openly.	6. Conflict should be handled discreetly and subtly.
7. Effective conflict management should be a problem-solving activity with a win-win outcome.	7. Effective conflict management should be a face-saving negotiation game with a win-win outcome.

2. *People interact with an intent to learn instead of an intent to protect themselves.*   You can learn a great deal about yourself, your partner, and your relationship if you approach conflict as a learning experience—one that will take your relationship forward instead of allowing it to stagnate or regress. Protecting yourself against conflict doesn't help a relationship grow.

3. *People do not stay stuck in conflict when the conflict is constructive.*   A destructive conflict, or series of conflicts, can make you feel stuck in one place within a relationship. Wilmot and Hocker point out that constructive conflict doesn't define who people are in a relationship; conflict is a dynamic process that emerges, plays out, and recedes.

4. *Constructive conflict enhances self-esteem in the participants.*   You probably don't associate conflict with enhanced self-esteem, because most of us think of conflict as negative and destructive. However, constructive conflict brings energy and productivity to a relationship and provides a more honest, complete picture of oneself.

5. *Constructive conflicts are characterized by a relationship focus instead of a purely individualistic focus.*   If parties in a conflict focus on the relationship instead of themselves, then the conflict will more likely be constructive than destructive. Participants should emphasize the "we" over the "I," so that conflict is seen as an experience that builds the relationship. If individual winning is more important than the relationship winning, then conflict will erode the relationship.

6. *Constructive conflict is primarily cooperative.*   Conflict built on competition, power struggles, and self-interest will destroy a relationship. Conversely, a cooperative, win–win approach to conflict will open the door for greater growth in a relationship.

Aware

Verbal

Conflict Involves Power   One of the most significant elements within interpersonal relationships is power. We might not realize it, but distributing power between partners requires a lot of subtle negotiation. Without this negotiation, conflict can become rampant. Furthermore, our ability to manage power successfully is a major factor in relational development. Power has been defined in a variety of ways, but for our purposes, **interpersonal power means the ability to influence another in the direction we desire—to get another person to do what we want.**[35] It also involves our ability to resist others' influences on us.[36] Perhaps it is easier to think of it in terms of who has more *control* in a relationship, rather than to use the term *power.*

All interactions, including conflicts, involve some level of power or control. If you ask a friend to go to a movie with you, you attempt to influence him or her. If the answer is no, your friend is mustering resistance and demonstrating power over you. If you don't like the negative response, you might attempt to assert control once more, perhaps by offering to buy your friend's ticket or to drive.

Romantic relationships can be typified by power dynamics.[37] **In what is termed a complementary relationship, one partner willingly and continuously cedes power to the other.** For example, a couple may feel completely comfortable with only one partner planning most of the activities, controlling the purse strings, and making decisions for the future of the relationship. Some partners prefer this arrangement because conflict doesn't arise over who wants control. However, the out-of-power partner may come to resent this status over time.

Symmetrical relationships are characterized by similar degrees of control on the part of each person. Both partners compete to dominate the other and assert control, or both relinquish control to the other to avoid making decisions or committing to something. In the first case, partners may argue over which television program to watch. In the second case, partners don't express preferences but engage in endless exchanges of "I don't know; whatever you want." The negotiation process can be time-consuming, fatiguing, and ineffective when quick decisions are needed.

In a **parallel relationship, power continually shifts from one partner to the other, depending on the nature of the interaction or situation.** One partner may take control because he or she is more experienced or equipped to handle a particular circumstance. This doesn't mean that one partner is constantly in an out-of-power position; rather, partners alternate being in control according to their strengths and weaknesses. For instance, if one partner is in charge of keeping the finances straight, she or he will have more power in budgetary decisions. If the other partner is a better cook, he or she probably will exert more power over decisions about diet and menus. This form of give and take works extremely well in intimate relationships, but partners need to agree on (and integrate into their self-concepts) who is really better suited to take control in certain situations. For example, when traveling by car, men and women often argue over directions to locations. (This may be a stereotype, but it's a stereotype many people experience.) Perhaps the man in the relationship believes that it is manly to be able to navigate, to know where one is going, and not to need to ask directions. However, when the couple ends up lost, they may find that the woman may actually be more adept at map-reading and navigating than the man. She may also be more comfortable stopping and asking for directions.

RECAP

Relationship Types Based on Power Dynamics

Relationship Type	Symbols	Explanation
Complementary	↑↓	One up, one down; one partner is almost always in power; the other is almost always out of power.
Symmetrical	↑↑↓↓	Both up or both down; partners either compete for power and control or relinquish power.
Parallel	→ ←	Give and take; power alternates between partners, depending on who is better equipped or more adept in certain situations.

Verbal

Conflict May Involve Assertive or Aggressive Communication

Sometimes our emotions cause us to communicate aggressively, when assertive communication would be preferable. You may tend to think of assertive and aggressive communication as being the same thing, but they are actually quite different. The best way to distinguish between the two is this: **Assertive communication takes the listener's feelings and rights into account; aggressive communication is self-serving and does not take the listener's feelings and rights into account**. Let's say that you experience a mix-up with a close friend over when and where you are supposed to meet. You get your signals crossed and don't end up going out together. When next you see your friend, you have the choice of responding to the frustration over the situation in a passive, assertive, or aggressive manner. You could be passive, say nothing about the mix-up, and simply "go along to get along." While this may sound like an unrealistic response, some people choose not to communicate even when they have been wronged. They are afraid of or unwilling to engage in any form of confrontation, no matter how benign or superficial, with strangers and intimates alike. A passive approach tends merely to internalize frustration, which may build into a destructive rage that at some point is bound to erupt.

Another option is to blow up at your friend. This is an aggressive, self-oriented approach because it does not take into account the rights of the recipient of such communication. Unfortunately, this is the tactic of choice for some people, especially if they have a great deal of anxiety and feel justified taking out their frustrations on others. An aggressive approach rarely achieves one's objectives.

Verbal aggression, also termed verbal abuse, has received much research attention in recent years, in an attempt to better understand the kind of threatening communication tactics persons in conflict occasionally resort to. Communication scholar Dominic Infante and various colleagues launched an interesting body of work on this topic, suggesting that verbal aggression is a form of communication violence because it attacks the heart of a person's being, her or his self-concept.[38] Conflicts that degenerate into verbal aggression can be characterized by insults ("You wouldn't say that if you had half a brain"), ridicule ("You're just too selfish to understand"), merciless teasing with an angry edge to it, character assassination ("You're low class"), and profanity.[39] Typically, the verbally aggressive person claims that the other person is the source or cause of the problem. Rather than focusing on the problem or the issues at hand, the verbally aggressive person shifts the focus to more personal issues.

We can more easily fend off verbal aggression from those who don't matter much to us, but we can be deeply wounded, and the relationship can be permanently damaged, by verbal aggression from someone important to us, whom we care about.[40] Unfortunately, verbally aggressive tactics are used widely in conflicts, according to research. One study surveyed dating partners and found that more than 70% reported using or experiencing some form of verbal aggression in their relational conflicts.[41] When the verbally aggressive tactics were used only occasionally—as lapses into "bad" behavior—partners were able to weather the aggression without much damage to the relationship. However, when the verbal aggression was more frequent, it signaled a relationship in trouble. Another study of verbal aggression among 5000 American college-age couples found that women and men are equally capable of producing verbally aggressive communication when in conflict.[42]

Infante and his associates have developed a measure that determines one's propensity for verbal aggression. However, one interesting finding from his research is that many persons who are deemed "highly verbally aggressive," as determined by the scale, don't characterize their behavior as such. Many believe their verbally aggressive comments in conflict situations to be humorous or benign kidding, not personal attacks that damage their relationships.[43] Research has also determined a connection between verbal aggression and physical aggression or abuse.[44]

Probably all of us, at some time or another, have been in a conflict situation with someone we cared about and we let a big, nasty, old "toad" fly out of our mouths. We probably felt terrible about it—maybe at the moment it flew out, or perhaps later, after we had time to reflect on the damage we'd done. As the research suggests, while it's not advisable or constructive for the relationship, occasional verbal aggression is likely to occur within a meaningful relationship. If you can remember some things you've said to someone that you wish you could take back, then you've had a moment of verbal aggression. But if you find that in a relationship with a romantic partner, close friend, family member, or even a coworker, verbally aggressive communication typifies your approach to conflict, then you definitely will want to spend some time thinking about why you tend to behave in an abusive manner. What is it about you— not the other person—that causes your communication to spiral downward and morph into a personal attack?

Clearly, an assertive approach is best—for ourselves and for the people we interact with. It's important to assert yourself and express your perception of a problem to the person who can best correct or clear it up rather than blowing off steam to an innocent bystander or third party. Communicating assertively means that you explain your concerns or cause for disagreement in a direct and firm manner, staying in control of your emotions but not allowing yourself to be bullied or discounted as you take the receiver's rights into account.

An assertive response to the timing mix-up with your friend might be something like this: "Hey, Joe, we were supposed to meet at five o'clock last night at the bowling alley, but you never showed up. What happened?" In this statement, you express your perception of the situation, but ask the person for his or her perception, rather than aggressively saying something in an angry tone that would make the other person defensive, such as "Why did you leave me hanging when we made definite plans?" If the person offers a lame excuse for not showing up, another assertive follow-up comment might be as follows: "Well, whatever happened, I just want you to know that I don't like being stood up; it's no big deal, but I just hope this doesn't happen again." If you

The best communicators haved learned to resolve conflict through the use of assertive rather than aggressive communication.

Aware

WATCH

communicate in this manner, you're far more likely to reach a positive resolution to any conflicts than if you behave passively or aggressively, violating the receiver's right to be treated humanely.[45]

Styles of Managing Conflict

Scholars in the communication discipline like to talk about conflict in terms of *management*, meaning that interpersonal communication can help people work through and handle conflict so that something positive results. What's your approach to managing interpersonal conflict: fight or flight? Do you tackle conflict head-on or seek ways to remove yourself from it? Most of us don't have a single way of dealing with disagreements, but we do have a tendency to manage conflict following patterns we learned early in life and have used before.[46] The pattern we choose depends on several factors, including our personality, the individuals with whom we are in conflict, and the time and place of the confrontation.

Researchers have attempted to identify styles of conflict management. One widely accepted approach organizes conflict styles into three types: (1) nonconfrontational; (2) confrontational or controlling; and (3) cooperative (also known as a *solution orientation*).[47]

Nonconfrontational Style   **One approach to managing conflict is to back off, either avoiding the conflict or giving in to the other person. Placating, distracting, computing, withdrawing, and giving in are responses that typify a** nonconfrontational style.

A *placating* response is an attempt to please; placaters are uncomfortable with negative emotions and may adopt this approach because they fear rejection if they rock the boat. Typically, they seek approval and try to avoid threats to their sense of self-worth. Placaters never seem to get angry, are so controlled that they seem unresponsive to the intensity of the situation, quickly agree with others to avoid conflict, and try to avoid confrontation at all costs.

Another nonconfrontational style is called *distracting.* Distracters attempt to change the subject or make a joke to avoid conflict or stress, rather than face issues directly. They hope that eventually the problem will just go away if it can be put off long enough.

A third nonconfrontational style is called *computing.* Computers remove themselves from conflict by remaining aloof and cool. They avoid emotional involvement and refuse to be provoked or ruffled, even under intense pressure. This detachment allows them to avoid expressing genuine feelings about issues and ideas. Instead, they respond to emotional issues with impersonal words and phrases, such as "One would tend to become angry when one's car is dented, wouldn't one?" The computing style is characterized by low empathy and minimal involvement with the issues at hand.

Withdrawing from conflict, either physically or psychologically, is another nonconfrontational approach. "I don't want to talk about it," "It's not my problem," and the one-word "Whatever" are typical responses from someone who uses this style.

Finally, some people consistently *give in* when faced with conflict. They are so uncomfortable that they surrender before the conflict escalates. Skip hates romantic movies. Yet when his girlfriend wants to rent *Must Love Dogs*, Skip agrees, just to avoid a conflict. A nonconfrontational or avoidant style often leads to a perpetuating conflict cycle that has a chilling or silencing effect on a relationship.[48] In addition, research shows that when conflict arises during problem-solving discussions, people who exhibit a nonconfrontational style of responding to the conflict are perceived as incompetent.[49]

"Well, if it doesn't matter who's right and who's wrong, why don't I be right and you be wrong?"

SIPRESS

Confrontational Style   Each of us has some need to control others, but some people always want to dominate and make sure that their objectives are achieved. In managing conflict, **people with a confrontational style have a win–lose philosophy. They want to win at the expense of the other person, to claim victory over their opponents, and to control others.** They focus on themselves and usually ignore the needs of others. Confronters often resort to blaming or seeking a scapegoat, rather than assuming responsibility for a conflict. "I didn't do it," "Don't look at me," and "It's not my fault" are typical responses. If this strategy doesn't work, confronters may try hostile name-calling, personal attacks, or threats.

Cooperative Style   **Those who have a cooperative style of conflict management view conflict as a set of problems to be solved, rather than a competition in which one person wins and another loses.** They work to foster a win–win climate by using the following techniques:[50]

- *Separate the people from the problem.*   Leave personal grievances out of the discussion. Describe problems without making judgmental statements about personalities.
- *Focus on shared interests.*   Emphasize common interests, values, and goals by asking such questions as "What do we both want?" "What do we both value?" "Where do we already agree?"

- *Generate many options to solve the problem.*   Use brainstorming and other techniques to generate alternative solutions.
- *Base decisions on objective criteria.*   Try to establish standards for an acceptable solution to a problem. These standards may involve cost, timing, and other factors.

RECAP

Conflict Management Styles

Nonconfrontational	A person avoids conflict by placating (agreeing), distracting, computing (becoming emotionally detached), withdrawing from conflict, or giving in to another person.
Confrontational	A person wants to manipulate others by blaming and making threats; sets up win–lose framework.
Cooperative	A person seeks mutually agreeable resolutions to manage differences; works within a win–win framework. • Separates people from problems • Focuses on shared interests • Generates many options to solve problems • Bases decisions on objective criteria

---

Conflict Management Skills

As we saw in the previous section, nonconfrontational and confrontational styles of conflict management do not solve problems effectively, nor do they foster healthy long-term relationships. The skills we review here are those we touched on in our discussion of the cooperative style.[51]

Managing conflict, especially emotionally charged conflict, is not easy. Even with a fully developed set of skills, you should not expect to melt tensions and resolve disagreements instantaneously. The following skills can, however, help you generate options that promote understanding and provide a framework for cooperation.

Manage Emotions   For weeks you have been working on a group project for an important class; your group has a firm deadline that the professor imposed. You submitted your portion of the project to your fellow group members two weeks ago. Today you check in with the group for a progress report and discover that very little has been done. The project is not much further along than when you completed your portion two weeks ago. Your grade is on the line;

you feel angry and frustrated. How should you respond? You may be tempted to march into the next group meeting and scream at your classmates. You might consider going to the professor and complaining about what has happened. Our best advice is this: Try to avoid taking action when you are in such an emotional state. You may regret what you say and you will probably escalate the conflict, making the situation worse.

Often the first sign that we are in a conflict situation is a combined feeling of anger, frustration, and fear that sweeps over us. Emotions that are aroused in us during conflict situations are understandable and to be expected. As psychotherapist Jeffrey Rubin explains, "Your feelings are your reality," meaning that the feelings conflict generates are real and should not be ignored.[52] In actuality, anger is not the predominant emotion generated by conflict. Many of us are unprepared for the aching, lonely, sad, and forlorn feelings that can emerge in conflict.[53] As tall an order as it is, it's important to try to understand the other person's feelings and to take the emotion of the situation seriously.

Expressing our feelings in an emotional outburst may make us feel better for the moment, but it also may exacerbate the situation and close the door to negotiation. Until we can tone down (not eliminate) and channel our emotions, we'll find it difficult to use appropriate communication skills to resolve conflict. Here are some specific strategies that you can draw on when an intense emotional response to conflict clouds your judgment and decision-making skills.[54]

WATCH

- *Select a mutually acceptable time and place to discuss a conflict.*   If you're upset or tired, you're at risk for an emotion-charged confrontation. If you ambush someone with an angry attack, you can't expect her or him to be in a productive frame of mind. Give yourself time to cool off before you try to resolve a conflict. In the case of the group project, you could call a meeting for later in the week. By that time, you could gain control of your feelings and think things through. Of course, sometimes issues need to be discussed on the spot; you may not have the luxury of waiting. But whenever it's practical, make sure your conflict partner is ready to receive you and your message and that you are prepared to present the message in a nonthreatening way.
- *Plan your message.*   If you approach someone to discuss a disagreement, take care to organize your message, even if that means organizing ideas on paper. Identify your goal and determine what outcome you would like; don't barge in unprepared and dump your emotions on the other person. You might also consider sounding things out with a trusted friend or colleague first, to check your perceptions and to help clarify the issues in the conflict.
- *Monitor nonverbal messages.*   Your nonverbal communication plays a key role in establishing an emotional climate. Monitor nonverbal messages— your own and those of others—to help defuse an emotionally charged

Verbal

Nonverbal

situation. Speak calmly, use direct eye contact, and maintain a calm facial expression and body position to signal that you wish to collaborate rather than control. Try also to place yourself on the same level as other people involved in the conflict. Standing while others sit, for example, can serve as a power cue and an impediment to resolving conflict.

- *Avoid personal attacks, name-calling, profanity, and emotional overstatement.*   Threats and derogatory language can turn a small conflict into an all-out war. When people feel attacked, they usually respond by becoming defensive in an effort to protect themselves. It's also important to avoid exaggerating your emotions. If you say you are irritated or annoyed rather than furious, you can still communicate your feelings, but you will take the sting out of your description. Avoid the bad habit of gunny-sacking—dredging up old problems and issues from the past (like pulling them out of an old bag or gunny sack) to use against your partner. Gunny-sacking usually succeeds only in increasing tension, escalating emotions, and reducing listening effectiveness. It's more helpful to keep everyone's focus on the issues at hand, not on old hurts from the past.

Aware

- *Use self-talk.*   Back to the problem of the group project: At the next meeting, what if a member lashes out at you, suggesting that you're a big part of the problem? Instead of lashing back at that person, the best advice would be to pause, take a slow, deep breath, and say to yourself, "I could get really mad, but that won't make things better. I'll respond calmly and coolly, so we keep the problem in proportion." You may think that talking to yourself is an eccentricity, but nothing could be further from the truth. Thoughts are directly linked to feelings; the messages we tell ourselves play a major role in how we feel and respond to others.[55]

Manage Information   Because uncertainty, misinformation, and misunderstanding are often byproducts of conflict and disagreement, skills that promote mutual understanding are important components of cooperative conflict management. The following skills can help you reduce uncertainty and enhance the quality of communication during conflict.

- *Clearly describe the conflict-producing events.*   Instead of blurting out complaints in random order, try to deliver a brief, well-organized presentation. Public speaking teachers recommend that, for certain speech topics, you describe events in chronological order. The same technique works well when describing a conflict. In our example of the group project situation, you could offer your perspective on what created the conflict, sequencing the events and describing them dispassionately so that your fellow group members end up sharing your understanding of the problem.

Verbal

- *"Own" your statements by using descriptive "I" language.*   In Chapter 1.3, we described the use of "I" language instead of "you" language in order to create a supportive climate. The same applies in conflict. "I feel upset when it seems like little is getting done and we're running the risk of not making our deadline." This is an example of an "I" statement that you could say to your group members. The statement describes your feelings as your own and keeps the issue manageable. Saying "You guys aren't pulling your weight and you're gonna blow our deadline" has an accusatory sting that will likely make members defensive, escalating the conflict. Also notice that, in the second statement, you don't take any responsibility for the problem but suggest that it belongs to several other people. This "ganging-up" approach almost always heightens people's defensiveness.

- *Use effective listening skills.* Managing information is a two-way process. Whether you are describing a conflict situation to someone or that individual is bringing a conflict to your attention, good listening skills are invaluable. Give your full attention to the speaker and make a conscious point of tuning out your internal messages. Sometimes the best thing to do after describing the conflict-producing events is simply to wait for a response. If you don't stop talking and give the other person a chance to respond, he or she will feel frustrated, the emotional pitch will go up a notch, and it will become more difficult to reach an understanding. Finally, not only should you focus on the facts or details, you should also analyze them so you can understand the major points the speaker makes. As Stephen Covey suggests in his book *The Seven Habits of Highly Effective People,* it is wise to "seek to understand rather than to be understood."[56]

- *Check your understanding of what others say and do.* Checking perceptions is vital when emotions run high. If you are genuinely unsure about facts, issues, or major ideas addressed during a conflict, ask questions to help you sort through them instead of barreling ahead with solutions. Then summarize your understanding of the information; don't parrot the speaker's words or paraphrase every statement, but check key points to ensure that you comprehend the message. Your response and that of your conflict partner will confirm that you understand each other.

On the Web

Perhaps you've heard, in the news or with regard to some incident that might have happened at work or school, of someone "going to mediation." As a new cottage industry, centers for mediation services are springing up with increasing frequency across the country. When people in conflict cannot resolve that conflict, they may turn to mediation before taking a more formal (and expensive) step, such as going to court.

Many universities now offer mediation services for students, faculty, and staff members. For example, the Ombuds Office at Stanford University defines mediation as a "voluntary meeting of disputing parties to attempt to reach their own solution with the help of a neutral person." The University of Virginia's mediation service was founded in 1996 to give students and community members an alternative for conflict resolution. This student-operated service is available only for students enrolled in the university. The Web site for Texas State University's Mediation Program quotes people who have used their mediation services for such situations as roommate grievances, problems within student organizations, and graduate student issues. This program engages trained faculty and staff from the university as mediators.

To read more about sample university mediation programs and services, visit these Web addresses:

www.vpfss.txstate.edu/personnel/mediation.htm
www.student.virginia.edu/~mediate
www.umich.edu/~sdrp
www.campus-adr.org
www.stanford.edu/dept/ocr/ombuds

Listen and Respond

Aware

Manage Goals As we have seen, conflict is goal driven. Both individuals involved in an interpersonal conflict want something. And, for some reason—

competitiveness, scarce resources, or lack of understanding—the goals appear to be in conflict. To manage conflict, it is important to seek an accurate understanding of these goals and to identify where they overlap. Here are a couple of techniques to help you accomplish just that.

Aware

Listen and Respond

- *Identify your goal and your partner's goal.*   After you describe, listen, and respond, your next task should be to identify what you would like to have happen. What is your goal? Most goal statements can be phrased in terms of wants or desires. Continuing with the group project example, you express to your fellow group members your goal of turning the project in on time. Next, it's useful to identify the goals of other people involved in the conflict. Use effective describing, listening, and responding skills to determine what each conflict partner wants. Obviously, if goals are kept hidden, it will be difficult to resolve the conflict.

- *Identify where your goals and your partner's goals overlap.*   Authorities on conflict negotiation stress the importance of focusing on shared interests when seeking to manage differences.[57] Armed with an understanding of what you want and what your partner wants, you can then determine whether the goals overlap. Suppose that after you explain your goal about the project deadline, another group member states that her or his goal is to make the project the best it possibly can be. These goals may be compatible, so you've identified a commonality that can help unify the group, rather than keep it splintered. But what if that goal of making the project the best means that your group will have to ask the professor for an extension on the deadline? Now you may have competing goals. But at least you've identified a central part of the problem. Framing the problem as "how can we achieve our mutual goal" rather than arguing over differences of opinion moves the discussion to a more productive level.

Adapt

Manage the Problem   If you can view conflicts as problems to be solved rather than battles to be won or lost, you will better manage the issues that confront you in your relationships with others. Of course, not all conflicts can be easily managed and resolved. But using a rational, logical approach to conflict management is more effective than emotionally flinging accusations and opinions at someone. Structuring a disagreement as a problem to solve helps manage emotions that often erupt; a problem-solving orientation to conflict also helps keep the conversation focused on issues rather than personalities. Once conflict becomes personal, people become defensive and emotions flare.

In the chapters ahead we suggest that the groups and teams that function most effectively use a structured approach to solving problems; ideas shouldn't just tumble over one another. A logical, organized approach usually works best when trying to solve vexing problems.

The problem-solving process is one you may have used in managing problems that have come your way. The approach is relatively simple: Define the problem, analyze the problem, generate possible solutions, evaluate the pros and cons of the solutions under consideration, and then select the solution that is agreeable to all concerned. The best solution is one that meets the goals of the persons involved in the conflict. As you apply the problem-solving approach to managing conflict, consider the following suggestions:

- *Resist developing solutions to manage the conflict until you and the other person fully understand the precise nature of the problem as well as each other's goals.*   When there is a problem to be solved, we typically want to head directly for solutions. Resist that temptation. Before blurting out solutions, realize that you're more likely to reach agreement on the solution to a problem if you each understand the specific issues that trigger the problem.
- *The more possible solutions you identify and consider, the greater the likelihood that the conflict will be managed successfully.*   If you're just batting around one or two solutions, you're limiting your options in managing the conflict. Rather than making the conflict a tug of war with only two ends of the rope pulling against each other, consider multiple creative strategies for achieving what you both want. Many people find it helps to make a written list of many possible ways to achieve each other's goals. The more options you discuss, the more likely it is that the two of you will find common ground.
- *Systematically discuss the pros and the cons of the possible solutions together.*   After you have a list of possible solutions, honestly identify advantages and disadvantages of each solution. How do you know which is the best solution? If you discussed the goals that each of you seek to achieve, you are well on your way to developing a vision of the future that can help you sort out the advantages and disadvantages of the potential solutions you're considering. Determine which solution, or combination of solutions, best achieves the goals you and your feuding partner are trying to accomplish.

We emphasize again that there are no sure-fire techniques that will manage or resolve the interpersonal conflicts that will inevitably occur even in the best of relationships. In reality, you don't simply manage your emotions and then march easily on to coolly communicate your ideas, followed by neatly sorting out goals and then rationally solving the problem that created the conflict. Conflict management is messier than this step-by-step process suggests. You may, for example, first try to manage your emotions, then communicate your ideas and feelings, only to find you need to go back and again manage your emotions. You are more than likely to bounce forward and backward from one step to another.

Our suggestions for managing emotions, information, goals, and the problem will not eliminate conflict from your life. Turning conflicts into problems to solve and seeking mutually agreeable solutions may, however, provide the necessary structure to help you manage conflict constructively.

PRINCIPLES FOR A LIFETIME: Enhancing Your Skills

Principle One: Be aware of your communication with yourself and others.

- Know your own interests, likes, and dislikes as you expand your circle of friends.
- Awareness and an understanding of self begin in your family as you grow up.
- Perception checking with colleagues increases your awareness of yourself and your workplace.
- The first stage of relational escalation, the pre-interaction awareness stage, begins with an awareness of the self and the other person to whom you are attracted.
- Even after relationships terminate, they still have an effect on our self-concept; be aware of the effect of relationships (even failed ones) on your view of yourself.
- It's important to know your conflict management style, especially if your style is different from that of other people involved in the conflict.
- Self-talk is appropriate in conflict, because it can help you manage your emotions and think clearly.
- Check your perceptions of a conflict with trusted others.
- Be aware of your own goals, as well as the goals of others, in conflict situations.

Aware

Principle Two: Effectively use and interpret verbal messages.

- Language patterns we learn as children in our families stay with us into adulthood.
- Persons in advanced stages of relationships tend to use verbal communication to discuss topics that typically are not discussed in early stages.
- Assertive communication takes the receiver's rights into account; aggressive communication does not.
- The management of the verbal expression of your emotions in conflict situations is an important skill.
- Plan your message carefully in a conflict situation.
- Avoid personal attacks, name-calling, profanity, and emotional overstatements in conflict situations.
- Use "I" language instead of "you" language in a conflict, so as to lessen defensiveness.

Verbal

Principle Three: Effectively use and interpret nonverbal messages.

- Nonverbal immediacy behaviors, such as eye contact and forward body lean, are important in the maintenance of friendships, family relationships, and workplace relationships.
- Persons in advanced stages of relationships tend to display nonverbal behaviors that typically are not in evidence in early stages.
- Nonverbal skills are important in your first conversations with people, as you attempt to establish and escalate relationships.
- Nonverbal immediacy cues diminish when a relationship is in de-escalation.
- Monitor and adapt your nonverbal behaviors in conflict situations.
- Monitor the nonverbal behaviors of other persons involved in your disagreement.

Nonverbal

Principle Four: Listen and respond thoughtfully to others.

- Listening is important in friendships, family relationships, and workplace relationships.
- Listening and responding appropriately are key skills potential employers value.
- Destructive conflict is characterized by a lack of listening.

Listen and Respond

- Conflict often escalates because the parties don't listen to one another; continue to listen, even if you feel yourself becoming emotional in the conflict.

Adapt

Principle Five: Appropriately adapt messages to others.

- It's important to learn to adapt our communication in friendships, family relationships, and workplace relationships.
- In conflict situations, partners often have to adapt to one another and admit that they were wrong. Destructive conflict often involves a reluctance to adapt to the other person and see the problem from her or his point of view.
- Be flexible and adapt to other cultures' approaches to conflict; don't assume that your home culture's approach to conflict management is applicable in conflicts with members of other cultural groups.
- After checking your perceptions of a conflict with trusted others, adapt your communication accordingly.
- One way to adapt in a conflict is to look for overlaps between your goals and the goals of your conflict partner.

SUMMARY

In this chapter we focused on interpersonal communication that enhances relationships and discussed three types of relationships that have tremendous impact on our lives: friendships, family relationships, and workplace relationships. We reviewed the five communication principles for a lifetime in light of each of these three forms of important relationships.

Most relationships develop in stages that are characterized by the type and presence (or absence) of interpersonal communication. Once relationships are initiated, they begin to escalate if the partners want the relationship to develop and become more intimate. Relationships also de-escalate as they move away from intimacy.

Conflict is a significant element within interpersonal relationships. The chapter distinguished between constructive and destructive conflict in relationships and explored six building blocks of constructive conflict. Power and control create patterns that can lead to harmony or strife in relationships. We also contrasted assertive communication (which takes receivers' rights into account) with aggressive communication (which ignores the rights of receivers). We examined three conflict management styles—nonconfrontational, confrontational, and cooperative—and discussed the forms of communication that characterize these styles. In a final section on conflict management skills, we suggested that you view conflicts as manageable events rather than as personal battles. We also offered suggestions for effective ways to manage emotions, information, goals, and problems, so that the resolution of conflict can actually make your relationships stronger.

DISCUSSION AND REVIEW

1. How does interpersonal communication facilitate the development of friendships? family relationships? workplace relationships?

2. What are the five stages of relational escalation? Do relationships necessarily have to go through each of the stages in order? What are the five stages of relational de-escalation? How do you prefer a relationship to end?

3. Define interpersonal conflict; provide examples of constructive and destructive conflicts.

4. A common issue faced by couples concerns shared activities, meaning who decides what the couple will and will not do together. How would a couple who have a complementary relationship (in terms of power) approach this issue? a symmetrical relationship? a parallel relationship?

5. What is the difference between assertive communication and aggressive communication? Provide an example of an aggressive response to someone's communication; then demonstrate how an assertive response would be preferable in the example.

6. What characterizes nonconfrontational, confrontational, and cooperative styles of conflict management?

PUTTING PRINCIPLES INTO PRACTICE

1. Think about your best friend, your closest family member, and a colleague (or classmate) with whom you feel close. Put the names of these three individuals across the top of a sheet of paper, forming columns down the page. Next, indicate in each column which forms of communication are most critical to the maintenance of each of these relationships. Finally, look for skills that appear in more than one column.

2. Work with a small group of classmates. Have each person think of a relationship—a friendship or romance—that has undergone the process of relational escalation and de-escalation. Discuss these processes and listen for commonalities in classmates' experiences. How did the quality of people's interpersonal communication move the relationship through the stages?

3. Sometimes it's hard to discern the difference between assertive and aggressive communication. To gain some practice, consider the following situations. For each one, first generate aggressive and inappropriate communication. Then rethink the situation and generate an assertive form of communication that would be more effective. We've provided an example to get you started.

   a. You are expecting a raise at work but find out that another coworker, who has less time on the job than you, received a raise and you did not.

      Aggressive Communication: You interrupt a staff meeting that your boss is holding, storm about the room and demand an explanation of why you did not receive the expected raise.

      Assertive Communication: You make an appointment with your boss for a meeting outside the office. At the meeting, you calmly ask the boss to assess your value to the company, leading up to the question of why you did not receive the expected raise.

   b. Two people have been in a monogamous dating relationship for several months when one partner finds out that the other person has cheated.

   c. A student receives a disappointing grade on a paper. After reading the papers of a few fellow classmates and finding that lesser quality papers received higher grades, the student decides to confront the teacher about the grade.

4. Generate an example of a common source of conflict for romantic couples. Then brainstorm ways that persons with nonconfrontational, confrontational, and cooperative styles of conflict management might approach the situation.

Chapter 2.2   *Practice Test*

MULTIPLE CHOICE. Choose the *best* answer to each of the following questions.

1. A conflict management style that seeks a win–win resolution is called
   a. cooperative.
   b. confrontational.
   c. nonconfrontational.
   d. passive.

2. When power in a romantic relationship continually shifts from one person to the other, the relationship is said to be
   a. complementary.
   b. symmetrical.
   c. parallel.
   d. elliptical.

3. Dr. Phil maintains that the following are all "truths" of verbal fighting *except*
   a. you can fight in a manner that will enhance your relationship.
   b. fighting in relationships is inevitable.
   c. fighting does not have to be painful.
   d. there are right and wrong ways to fight.

4. Lola says to her romantic partner, "I don't think we should see each other as much. I need to spend more time with my friends and I am getting behind in school. Maybe we can see each other just on the weekends." From her talk, it appears the relationship is entering which stage of relationship de-escalation?
   a. de-intensification stage
   b. intensification stage
   c. separation stage
   d. post-interaction stage

5. _____ communication takes into consideration the listener's feelings and rights.
   a. Passive
   b. Assertive
   c. Aggressive
   d. Complementary

6. Friendships with peers have their greatest impact during
   a. childhood.
   b. adolescence.
   c. adulthood.
   d. old age.

7. According to the model presented in the textbook, a romantic couple would engage in which stage of relationship development first?
   a. initiation
   b. intimacy
   c. pre-interaction awareness
   d. intensification

8. In an intimate relationship that is not going well, the partners typically
   a. end the relationship at the current stage.
   b. progress back through the stages they have already experienced.
   c. enter a turmoil or stagnation stage.
   d. merely reverse the escalation process.

9. According to Hughes and her colleagues, friends-with-benefits operate according to which of the following rules?
   a. Emotions can be involved until someone starts dating another person.
   b. The relationship can exist only so long as neither person has another sexual/romantic partner.
   c. The original friendship and activities remain the same and are not changed by sexual activity.
   d. Only the closest of friends are allowed to know about the sexual nature of the friendship.

10. Those in individualistic cultures believe that conflict
   a. should be handled directly and openly.
   b. can only be dysfunctional.
   c. should deal with substantive and relational issues together.
   d. should result in a winner and a loser.

11. In ending a relationship, most people prefer
   a. an abrupt or definite breakup.
   b. a general fading away.
   c. a final and ultimate conflict.
   d. to end things face to face.

12. According to Virginia Satir, healthy families tend to have all of the following characteristics *except*
   a. a high sense of self-worth.
   b. flexible rules.
   c. honest communication.
   d. clear and strict rules.

13. Martha has just shown up for her first day at work. In all likelihood, she will use which strategy for reducing uncertainty?
   a. passive
   b. active
   c. interactive
   d. transactive

14. According to William Wilmot and Joyce Hocker, constructive conflict
   a. involves protecting yourself against situations where conflict might arise.
   b. demands a more rigid approach to relationships.
   c. focuses on finding a winner of the conflict.
   d. emphasizes learning instead of self-protection.

15. When one person in a romantic relationship continually allows the other to have most of the power, the relationship is said to be
   a. complementary.
   b. symmetrical.
   c. parallel.
   d. elliptical.

16. Dominic Infante's research has determined that people who are highly verbally aggressive
   a. recognize their aggressiveness and want to find ways of diminishing it.
   b. recognize their aggressiveness and do not want to change it.
   c. view their aggressiveness as an asset and wish they were even more aggressive.
   d. view their aggressiveness mainly as humorous.

17. Having found a number of common interests, Gavin and Mason begin to talk more in depth about their beliefs and values. They have also begun to use "we" and "us" when they talk and occasionally engage in intimate touch. Which stage of relational escalation describes their relationship?
   a. exploration
   b. individualization
   c. intensification
   d. intimacy

18. With regard to Barbie and Ken's breakup, a Mattel spokesman stated that it was "time to spend some quality time apart," though they would remain friends. This statement is an example of
   a. placating.
   b. distracting.
   c. grave-dressing.
   d. computing.

19. The main difference between assertive and aggressive communication is
   a. nonverbal, mainly based on tone and volume of speech.
   b. that assertive communication focuses on the other person's feelings and not your own.
   c. that assertive communication focuses on your own feelings and not the other person's feelings.
   d. that assertive communication focuses on your own feelings and considers the other's feelings.

20. According to your authors, "the more possible _____ you identify and consider, the greater the likelihood that the conflict will be managed successfully."
   a. feelings
   b. causes
   c. solutions
   d. goals

TRUE/FALSE. Indicate whether the following statements are *true* or *false*.

1. T or F   In a collectivist culture, conflict is considered destructive to relational harmony.

2. T or F   Conflicts are best managed at the time the disagreement occurs.

3. T or F   Using confrontational styles of conflict management guarantees that the conflict will be resolved constructively.

4. T or F   Highly personalized communication occurs during the intimacy stage of a relationship.

5. T or F   All relationships proceed through the stages of escalation and de-escalation at the same rate.

6. T or F   Women and men are equally capable of verbal aggression in conflict.

7. T or F   Focusing on satisfying individual needs is more likely to lead to constructive conflict.

8. T or F   By and large, anger is the most common emotion generated by conflict.

9. T or F   In order to keep conflict constructive, it is best not to express emotions when managing it.

10. T or F   Before choosing a solution to a conflict, it is best to discuss the pros and cons of the possible solutions together.

FILL IN THE BLANK. Complete the following statements.

1. Partners who engage in cooperative approaches to resolving their differences are using _____ conflict.

2. The relational development stages of pre-interaction awareness, initiation, exploration, intensification, and intimacy make up relational _____.

3. Any struggle between two people who cannot agree on a way to meet their needs is interpersonal _____.

4. _____ conflict damages relationships because partners lack cooperation in dealing with their differences.

5. Interpersonal _____ is the ability to influence another person.

6. Approaching conflict with a win–win approach is characteristic of the _____ style.

7. _____ communication is self-serving and does not take into account the rights of the other person.

8. Dealing with conflict by backing off or avoiding it outright is an example of a _____ style.

9. Attempting to control conflict to ensure that one person wins and the other loses is an example of a _____ style.

10. The relational development stages of turmoil, de-intensification, individualization, separation, and post-interaction make up relational _____.

Interviewing

APPENDIX OBJECTIVES

After studying this appendix, you should be able to

1. Describe what an interview is.

2. Identify five different kinds of interview goals.

3. Identify and discuss the important elements of being interviewed for a job.

4. Develop a clear, well-worded resumé.

5. Identify and discuss the important elements of participating in an information-gathering interview.

6. Explain how to conduct an interview.

The stakes are often high when you participate in an interview. If you are interviewing for a job, your career and perhaps your future rest on the impression you make. If someone is interviewing you to gather information, the accuracy of what you say can have a powerful impact on others. Or if you are the person who is conducting the job interview, you have much to gain or lose; your choice of a new employee will affect the success of the organization. If you're interviewing someone to gather information, your credibility is at stake if you pass on or publish information that later proves to be false or inaccurate.

In this introduction to interviewing, we'll discuss communication strategies that can enhance your job interview skills and offer tips about how to participate in an information-gathering interview. We conclude the appendix by identifying strategies that can help you polish your talents if you are the person interviewing others. Whether you are a recent high school graduate or have been in the work force for several years and have come back to school to finish your degree and pursue a new career, the principles for a lifetime that we've emphasized in this book can help you enhance your interviewing skills.

The Nature and Types of Interviews

An interview is a form of oral interaction structured to achieve a goal, which often involves just two people, but could include more than two people, who take turns speaking and listening. An effective interview is not a random conversation but occurs when the person conducting the interview has carefully framed the objectives of the interview and developed a structured plan for achieving the objectives. The person being interviewed should also prepare by considering the kinds of questions he or she may be asked and being ready to give appropriate responses.

When many people think of the term *interview*, the most common image that comes to mind is a job interview. Yet interviews can also be means of gathering information, sharing job performance feedback, solving problems, and persuading others. Even though we are focusing primarily on employment and information-gathering interviews, the strategies we present can help you with *any* interview situation.

Information-Gathering Interview

Information-gathering interviews, just as the name suggests, **are designed to seek information from the person being interviewed.** Public-opinion polls are one type of information-gathering interview. When you leave an organization, you may be asked to participate in an exit interview, an interview designed to assess why you are leaving the company. A reporter for a newspaper, radio, or TV station interviews people to gather information for a story or broadcast.

Those most skilled at conducting information-gathering interviews do their homework before the interview. They come prepared with specific questions and have already conducted background research. In addition to preparing questions, a skilled information-gathering interviewer listens and develops questions that stem from the information that is shared during the interview.

Appraisal Interview

An appraisal interview, sometimes called a performance review, **occurs when a supervisor or employer shares information with you about your job performance.** Such an interview enables you to see how others perceive your effectiveness and helps you determine whether you are likely to get a promotion or a "pink slip." During an appraisal interview you can typically express your observations about the organization and your goals for the future.

Usually a supervisor begins by preparing a written report summarizing your strengths and weaknesses, then meets with you to review it.

When receiving feedback from a supervisor, the best approach is to listen and gather as much objective information about his or her perceptions as possible. In an evaluation situation, especially if the feedback is negative, it is easy to become defensive; try to manage your emotions and use the information to your benefit instead. If you disagree with your supervisor's evaluation, consider using the conflict management skills we discussed in Chapter 2.2. In addition, provide specific examples to support your position. Just saying you don't like the review is likely to do more harm than good.

Problem-Solving Interview

A **problem-solving interview is designed to resolve a problem that affects one or both parties involved in the interview**. A disciplinary interview to consider corrective action toward an employee or student is one type of problem-solving interview. Grievance interviews are also problem-solving interviews; one person brings a grievance or complaint against another person, and solutions are sought to resolve the problem or conflict.

The strategies for structuring a problem-solving group discussion that we present in Chapter 3.2 can also help you organize a problem-solving interview. Before seeking to solve or manage a problem, first define the issues and then analyze the causes, history, and symptoms of the problem. Rather than focusing on only one solution, brainstorm several possible solutions and then evaluate the pros and the cons of the potential solutions before settling on a single solution.

Persuasion Interview

During a **persuasion interview, one person seeks to change or reinforce the attitudes, beliefs, values, or behavior of another person.** The sales interview is a classic example of an interview in which the goal is to persuade. A political campaign interview is another example of a persuasion interview.

Our discussion in Chapter 4.5 of the principles and strategies of persuading others can help you prepare for a persuasion interview. The advantage of trying to persuade someone during an interview rather than in a speech is the size of the audience; during a persuasive interview, you may have an audience of one. It is especially important to analyze and adapt to your listener when seeking to persuade.

Job Interview

A **job interview is a focused, structured conversation whose goal is to assess the credentials and skills of a person for employment.** The job interview may involve elements of each of the types of interviews we've already discussed. Information is both gathered and shared; it will certainly solve a problem if you're the one looking for a job and you are hired. Elements

By using all the commu-
nication skills you have
learned in this course,
you just might land that
all-important first job.

of persuasion are also involved in a job interview. If you are seeking a job, you're trying to persuade the interviewer to hire you; if you are the interviewer and you're interviewing an exceptionally talented person, your job is to persuade the interviewee to join your organization.

The planned or structured nature of an interview sets it apart from other communication situations. Yet interviews may sometimes include elements of interpersonal, group, and presentational communication. Interviews embody interpersonal communication in that there are two or more people participating in the interview who must establish a relationship. If the goal of the interview is to find a solution to a vexing problem, the interview may resemble elements of a group discussion in which a problem is defined and analyzed and solutions are generated, evaluated, and then implemented. Preparing for a job interview is like a public speaking situation; you focus on your audience (the interviewer), keep your purpose in mind as you research the company you're interviewing with, organize your ideas, and even rehearse your responses to questions you think you may be asked.

Regardless of the purpose or format of an interview, the five communication principles for a lifetime that we've used to organize our discussion of interpersonal, group and team, and presentational communication situations will serve you well when you participate in an interview. Whether you are the interviewer or the interviewee, it is important to be aware of how you are coming across to others. Using and interpreting verbal and nonverbal messages are critical to participating in a successful interview. In our definition of an interview, we noted that all individuals involved both talk and listen. Unless you can adapt your messages to others, you won't be successful. Effective interview participants are able to listen, respond, and speak extemporaneously, rather than delivering overly scripted, planned messages. Adapting to others is essential.

Aware
Verbal
Nonverbal
Listen and Respond
Adapt

Interview Structure

Just as a speech or term paper has a beginning, middle, and end, so does a well-structured interview. Most interviews have three phases:

1. *The opening.*　The interviewer tries to put the interviewee at ease and presents an overview of the interview agenda.
2. *The body.*　During the longest part of an interview, the interviewer asks questions, and the interviewee listens and responds. The interviewee may also ask questions.
3. *The conclusion.*　The interviewer summarizes what will happen next and usually gives the interviewee an opportunity to ask any final questions.

It is the responsibility of the person leading the interview to develop a structure for the interview. But it's helpful for the interviewee to understand the overall structure of an interview in advance in order to know what to expect both before and during the interview. So, whether you're the interviewer (regardless of the type of interview) or the interviewee, understanding the interview structure we discuss should be of value to you.

The Opening

The opening of any interview is crucial because it creates a climate for positive and open communication. When interviewing someone, you should strive to establish rapport and clarify the goals of the interview.

To establish rapport, start the conversation with something that will put the interviewee at ease. The discussion could be about something as simple as the weather, recent events both of you attended, or other light topics. Making direct eye contact, smiling appropriately, and offering a firm handshake all help establish a warm atmosphere.

Besides making the interviewee comfortable, the interviewer should clarify the goals of the interview by explicitly stating the general purpose for the meeting. After the opening conversation, it may be helpful to provide a general overview of the nature and purpose of the interview and an estimate of how long the interview will last. Clarifying a meeting's purpose helps both parties get their bearings and check their understanding. A good interviewer makes sure that everyone is on the same wavelength before the actual questioning begins.

Arrive for the interview a few minutes ahead of the scheduled hour. Be prepared, however, to wait patiently, if necessary. If you are the interviewer and have decided to use a recorder, set it up. You may keep it out of sight once the interviewee has seen it, but *never* try to hide a recorder at the outset—such a ploy is unethical and illegal. If you are going to take written notes, get out your paper and pen. Now you are ready to begin asking your prepared questions.

The Body: Asking Questions

Once the interviewee is at ease during the opening of the interview, the bulk of the interview will consist of the interviewer asking the interviewee questions. If an interviewer has done a good job of identifying and clarifying his or her objectives and gathering information, the key questions to be asked usually are fairly obvious. But what kinds of questions are they?

Question Types   An interview is conducted as a series of questions and responses. Even though both parties listen and speak, the interviewer has the primary responsibility for questioning. Interview questions fall into one of four categories: open, closed, probing, or hypothetical.[1] A typical interview usually includes some of each type.

Open Questions   **Open questions are broad and basically unstructured. Often they indicate only the topic to be considered and allow interviewees considerable freedom to determine the amount and kind of information they will provide.**

Because they encourage the interviewee to share information almost without restriction, open questions are useful to determine opinions, values, and perspective. Such questions as "What are your long- and short-term career goals?" or "Why do you seek employment here?" or "How do you feel about gun control?" prompt personal and wide-ranging responses.

Closed Questions   **Closed questions limit the range of possible responses.** They may ask for a simple yes or no—"Do you enjoy working in teams?"—or they may allow interviewees to select responses from a number of specific alternatives: "How often do you go to the movies? (1) Less than once a month, (2) Once a month, (3) Twice a month, (4) Once a week." Closed questions enable the interviewer to gather specific information, by restricting interviewees' freedom to express personal views or elaborate on responses. Closed questions are most often used when an interviewer is trying to obtain a maximum amount of information in a short period of time.

Probing Questions   **Probing questions encourage interviewees to clarify or elaborate on partial or superficial responses.** Through the use of these questions, interviewers attempt to clarify or direct responses. Such questions as "Could you elaborate on your coursework in the area of communication?" "Do you mean to say that you already own three vacuum cleaners?" and "Will you tell me more about your relationship with your supervisor?" call for further information in a particular area. Often spontaneous, probing questions follow up on the key questions that interviewers have prepared in advance.

Hypothetical Questions   **Interviewers use hypothetical questions to describe a set of conditions and ask interviewees what they would do if they were in those situations. Such questions are generally used**

either to gauge reactions to emotion-arousing or value-laden circumstances or to reveal an interviewee's likely responses to real situations. A police officer might ask an eyewitness to a murder, "What if I told you that the man you identified as the murderer in the line-up was the mayor?" During an exit interview, a personnel manager might ask, "If we promoted you to Chief Sanitary Engineer and paid you $4 an hour more, would you consider staying with Bob's Landfill and Television Repair?"

RECAP

Types of Interview Questions

	Uses	Example
Open Question	Prompts wide-ranging responses. Answers reveal interviewee's opinions, values, perspectives.	Tell me about your previous job duties. How would you describe your son's problems in school?
Closed Question	Requests simple yes or no response or forces interviewee to select a response from limited options.	Have you been skiing in the past month? Which one of the following drinks would you buy? a. Coke b. Pepsi c. 7-Up
Probing Question	Encourages clarification of or elaboration on previous responses. Directs responses in a specific direction.	Would you tell me more about the pain in your side? We've talked about your mother. Can you describe how you felt about your father's long absences from home when you were a child?
Hypothetical Question	Gauges reactions to emotional or value-laden situations. Elicits response to a real or imaginary situation.	How would you support your opponent if she were elected chair of the board? What would you do if your secretary lost an important file?

FIGURE A.1
The Funnel Sequence

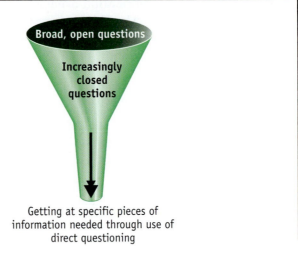

Broad, open questions

Increasingly closed questions

Getting at specific pieces of information needed through use of direct questioning

Questioning Sequences   Open, closed, probing, and hypothetical questions may be used in any combination, as long as their sequence is thoughtfully planned. Depending on the purpose, these questions may be arranged into three basic sequences: funnel, inverted funnel, and tunnel.

The Funnel Sequence   The **funnel sequence begins with broad, open questions and proceeds to more closed questions** (see Figure A.1). The advantage of this format is that it allows an interviewee to express views and feelings without restriction, at least early in an interview. For example, it may be more useful to begin a grievance interview with the question "How would you describe your relationship with your supervisor?" instead of asking "What makes you think your supervisor treats you like an idiot?" The first question allows the free expression of feelings, while the second question clearly reflects an interviewer's bias, immediately forcing the discussion in a negative direction. The following series of questions provides an example of a funnel sequence that might be used for an information-gathering interview.

1. Why do you find communication interesting?
2. What area of communication are you primarily interested in?
3. How long have you studied interpersonal communication?
4. Why do you think interpersonal attraction theory is useful?
5. What would you do to test interpersonal attraction theory?

Notice that the questions start by asking for general information and then focus on more specific ideas.

The Inverted Funnel Sequence   Just the opposite of the funnel sequence, **the inverted funnel sequence begins with closed questions and proceeds to more open questions** (Figure A.2). An interview designed to

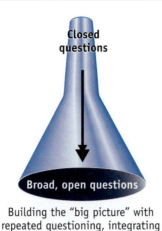

Closed
questions

Broad, open questions

Building the "big picture" with
repeated questioning, integrating
previous responses

FIGURE A.2
The Inverted Funnel
Sequence

gather information about a worker grievance might be based on the inverted funnel and might include the following series of questions:

1. Do you believe that your supervisor wants to fire you?
2. What makes you think you'll be fired soon?
3. What do you think has caused this problem between you and your supervisor?
4. How has this problem affected your work?
5. How would you describe the general working climate in your department?

The relatively closed questions that begin the inverted funnel sequence are intended to encourage an interviewee to respond easily, because they require only brief answers (yes or no, short lists, and the like). As the sequence progresses, the questions become more open and thus require more elaborate answers and greater disclosure.

The inverted funnel sequence is appropriate when an interviewer wants to direct the interview along specific lines and encourage an interviewee to respond with short, easily composed answers. An interviewer can follow up with more general questions to provide increasingly broad information—the "big picture," so to speak.

The Tunnel Sequence   Finally, **the tunnel sequence consists of a series of related open or closed questions or a combination of the two; the sequence is intended to gather a wide range of information.** This sequence does not include probing questions; it goes into less depth than the other two sequences. An interviewer may use the tunnel sequence to gather information about attitudes and opinions without regard for the reasons behind an interviewee's answers or the intensity of his or her feelings. The following is a typical tunnel sequence:

1. What are the three major issues in the presidential campaign this year?
2. Which candidate would you vote for if the election were held today?

3. For whom do you think you will vote in the race for U.S. Senator?
4. Are you a registered voter in this state?
5. What do you think of the proposition to set up a nuclear waste dump in this state?

The tunnel sequence is most appropriate when an interviewer wants some general information on a variety of topics in a relatively short period of time.

Although these sequences have been discussed as if they were independent and easily distinguishable, good questioning strategy will probably combine one or more question sequences. The key to effective interviewing is to prepare a set of questions that will get the needed kinds and amount of information. An interviewer should remain flexible enough to add, subtract, and revise questions as a discussion proceeds. Such an approach ensures that the objectives of the interview will be accomplished.

As you conduct the interview, use the questions you have prepared as a guide but not a rigid schedule. If the person you are interviewing mentions an interesting angle you did not think of, don't be afraid to pursue the point. Listen carefully to the person's answers, and ask for clarification of any ideas you don't understand.

The Conclusion

Opinion polls, marketing surveys, and sales pitches often end rather abruptly with a "Thank you for taking the time to help me out." Many other kinds of interviews require follow-up meetings or some form of future contact, however. For this reason, and for reasons of common courtesy, the conclusion of an interview is very important.

A primary function of the conclusion is to summarize the proceedings. All parties should be aware of and agree on what happened during the meeting. To ensure understanding and agreement, an interviewer summarizes the highlights of the discussion, asking for and offering clarification, if necessary.

Another function of the conclusion is to encourage continued friendly relations. The positive communication climate developed during the interview should be carried into the conclusion. You may need to establish interpersonal harmony if you asked questions that resulted in conflict or made the interviewee uncomfortable. Comments such as "I'm glad we had a chance to talk about this problem" or "Thank you for sharing and listening" enable both parties to feel that they have had a positive and productive encounter. An interviewer can tell the other person when to expect further contact or action, if appropriate. A job applicant wants to know when to expect a phone call about a follow-up interview or a job offer. An expert, interviewed by a journalist, wants to know what will be done with her comments and when the story is likely to be published.

At the end of virtually any interview, good manners require both the interviewer and the interviewee to say "Thank you." Because an interview is a mutual effort, both parties deserve recognition. One final suggestion: Do not prolong the interview beyond the time limits of your appointment.

RECAP

Organizing an Interview

Step	Goals
Opening	Put the interviewee at ease.
	Review the purpose.
	Establish rapport.
	Provide an orientation.
Body	Use questions appropriate to the interview type and objective.
	• Use open questions to elicit wide-ranging responses.
	• Use closed questions to get specific responses.
	• Use probing questions to seek clarification or elaboration.
	• Use hypothetical questions to gauge a reaction to an imaginary situation.
	Design questioning sequences appropriate to the interview purpose.
	• Use the funnel sequence to elicit general comments first and specific information later.
	• Use the inverted funnel sequence to elicit specific information first and more general comments later.
	• Use the tunnel sequence to gather lots of information without probing too deeply.
Conclusion	Summarize the proceedings.
	Encourage friendly relations.
	Arrange further contact(s).
	Exchange thank-yous.

How to Be Interviewed for a Job

It's been said that a major element in being successful in life is just showing up—but we suggest that you do more than just show up for a job interview. Giving a speech involves considerable preparation. Like a speech, a successful job interview involves thoughtful preparation and careful planning.

Be Aware of Your Skills and Abilities

The first communication principle we introduced in this book is to be aware of your communication. Before you interview for a job, it is important to be aware

EXPLORE

Aware

not only of your communication as you interact with others, but also of your unique skills, talents, and abilities. Many people select a career because they think they might like to *be* a lawyer, doctor, or teacher. But rather than thinking about what you want to be, we suggest considering what you like to *do*. Ask yourself these questions:

- What do I like to do in my free time?
- What are my best skills and talents?
- What education and training do I have?
- What experiences or previous jobs have I had?

In addition to these questions, write down responses to complete this statement: "I can . . . ." For example, you might respond: "I can cook, write, relate well to others." List as many answers as possible. Here's another statement to complete: "I have . . . ." "I have traveled, worked on a farm, sold magazine subscriptions." Responding to the "I can" and "I have" statements will help you develop an awareness of your skills and experiences that will help you respond readily when you are asked about them during the interview. Reflecting on your interests can help you decide which career will best suit your talents; you will also be able to develop a resumé that reflects your best abilities.

Verbal

Prepare Your Resumé

A resumé is a written, concise, well-organized description of your qualifications for a job. How long should a resumé be? Many employers don't expect a resumé to be longer than two pages; some will look only at a one-page resumé. (Resumés of experienced career professionals may be longer than two pages, however.) Although your resumé is important in helping you land a job, its key function is to help you get an interview—it's how you perform in the interview that determines whether you get the job. Employers rarely hire someone based only on a resumé. Most employers spend less than a minute—and some only a few seconds—looking at each resumé. Therefore, your resumé should be clear and easy to read and should focus on the essential information an employer seeks.

Most employers will be looking for standard information on your resumé. Study the sample resumé that appears on the next page.[2] Here's a list of the essential pieces of information that should be included on your resume.

- *Personal information.*   Employers will look for your name, address, phone numbers, e-mail address, and a Web page address (if you have one). Provide phone numbers where you can be reached during both the day and the evening.
- *Career objective.*   Many employers will want to see your career objective. Make it brief, clear, and focused. You may need to customize your career objective for the different positions you seek.
- *Education.*   Include your major, your degree, your graduation date, and the institution you attended.

SAMPLE RESUMÉ

Mark Smith
3124 West Sixth Street
San Marcos, TX 78666
(512)555-0102
(512)555-0010

PROFESSIONAL OBJECTIVE: Seeking a position in human resources as a training specialist.

EDUCATION:
Bachelor of Arts degree
Major: Communication Studies
Minor: English
Texas State University–San Marcos
Graduation date: May 20XX

PROFESSIONAL EXPERIENCE:

20XX–Present, Intern, GSD&M, Austin, Texas. Assisted in creating a leadership training program. Wrote copy for flyers and display ads. Made cold calls to prospective clients. Position required extensive use of desktop publishing programs.

20XX–August 20XX, Intern, Target Market, Houston, Texas. Developed sales training seminar. Coordinated initial plan for writing advertising copy for Crest Inc.'s advertising campaign.

20XX–20XX, Supervisor, S&B Associates, San Marcos, Texas. Supervised three employees editing training materials.

20XX–20XX, Advertising Sales and Reporter, *University Star*, San Marcos, Texas. Sold ads for university paper and worked as social events reporter.

OTHER EXPERIENCES: 20XX–20XX, Summer jobs and part-time work.

SKILLS: 20XX–20XX, Team Leadership, Photography, Computer Proficiency, Research and Analysis, Public Speaking, Customer Service.

ACCOMPLISHMENTS AND HONORS: Paid for majority of my college education while maintaining a 3.5 grade point average, Presidential Scholarship, Vice President of Texas State University Communication Club, Editor/Historian of MortarBoard, John Marshall High School Vice President of Junior Class, Yearbook Coordinator.

PROFESSIONAL ORGANIZATIONS: Lambda Pi Eta, American Society for Training and Development, Communication Club, National Communication Association.

INTERESTS: Photography, tennis, softball, theatre.

REFERENCES: Available at your request.

- *Experience.*   Describe your relevant work experience, listing your most recent job first. Include the names of employers, dates when you worked, and a very brief description of your duties.
- *Honors and special accomplishments.*   List any awards, honors, offices held, or other leadership responsibilities.
- *Optional information.*   If you have volunteer experience, have traveled, or have computer skills or other pertinent experience, be sure to include it if it is relevant to your objective and the job.
- *References.*   List the names, phone and fax numbers, and e-mail addresses of people who can speak positively about your skills and abilities. Or you may indicate that your references are available on request.

When developing your resumé, be sure to use specific action verbs to describe your experience. Also use these action words during your interview. Rather than using a general verb such as "I *worked* on a project," use more descriptive action words that clarify the role you assumed. Consider using some of the following words when listing or describing your activities or accomplishments:

accelerated	evaluated	planned
accepted	expanded	promoted
accomplished	expedited	proposed
achieved	facilitated	provided
adapted	found	recommended
administered	generated	reduced
analyzed	guided	researched
approved	improved	resulted in
built	increased	reviewed
completed	influenced	revised
conceived	initiated	selected
conducted	instructed	solved
controlled	interpreted	stimulated
coordinated	maintained	structured
created	managed	supervised
delegated	mastered	tested
demonstrated	motivated	trained
designed	negotiated	translated
developed	operated	traveled
directed	organized	updated
effected	originated	utilized
eliminated	participated	won

Identify the Needs of Your Employer

After you have analyzed your skills and abilities and prepared a well-crafted resumé, you need to be audience centered, to anticipate the needs and goals of your potential employer. A good interviewee adapts his or her message to the interviewer.

How do you find out information about an organization that will help you adapt your message to fit the needs of the organization? In a word, research. Gather as much information as you can about not only the person who will interview you but the needs and goals of the organization or company where you seek a job. Most libraries include books and articles about organizations both large and small. Typical library resources that have information about major corporations include

Adapt

- *The Information Please Business Almanac and Sourcebook*
- *Louis Rukeyser's Business Almanac*
- *Standard and Poor's Register of Corporations, Directors, and Executives*
- *The Job Vault: The One-Stop Job Search Resource*

Virtually every organization these days has a Web page. Explore the information available on the Web. Do more than just look at the organization's home page; explore the various hyperlinks that help you learn about what the organization does.

What determines whether you are hired for the job? The short answer to this question is "the way you communicate." By the time you get to an interview, your interviewer has already determined that you have at least minimum qualifications for the job. Your ability to apply the communication principles for a lifetime that we've reiterated throughout the book is key to making a good impression on your interviewer. In Chapter 1.1, when discussing why it's important to learn about communication, we noted the key factors that employers look for in a job applicant; the top three factors focus on your communication skill.[3] Your ability to listen, respond, and relate to your interviewer is one of the best predictors of whether you will be hired for a job.

As you prepare for the interview, don't forget about the power of nonverbal messages in making a good impression, which we discussed in Chapter 1.4. Dressing for success is important. Most experts suggest you dress conservatively and give special attention to your grooming. For most professional positions, men will be expected to wear a coat and tie or a suit and well-polished shoes. Women will be expected to wear a dress, suit, or other coordinated attire.

Nonverbal

Besides assessing your appearance and your ability to communicate, interviewers consider several other traits:

- *Self-expression.*   Are you clear or vague when you respond to questions? Do you have effective eye contact? Do you talk too much or too little?
- *Maturity.*   Are you likely to make good judgments and effective decisions?
- *Personality.*   What's your overall style of relating to people? Are you outgoing, shy, quiet, overbearing, enthusiastic, warm, friendly?
- *Experience.*   Can you do the job? Do you have a track record that suggests you can effectively do what needs to be done?
- *Enthusiasm.*   Do you seem interested in this job and the organization? Do you seem to be genuine and authentic, or is your enthusiasm phony?

Listen and Respond

- *Goals.*   Where are you heading in life? Are your short-term and long-term goals compatible with the needs of the organization?

Listen, Respond, and Ask Appropriate Questions

Listen and Respond

Because an interview is a structured, planned discussion, it is important to demonstrate effective listening and responding skills. Stay focused on what your interviewer is asking you. Remember to stop, look, and listen for both the details of the questions and the major points of the questions.

When you respond to questions, you should project genuine enthusiasm and competence. Don't put on an act: be yourself while being professional. Be friendly and pleasant without being overly effusive or giddy.

One of the best ways to prepare for an interview is to anticipate the interviewer's questions. Table A.1 lists typical questions that may be asked during an interview. We don't recommend that you memorize "canned" or overly rehearsed answers, but it may be helpful to think about possible responses to these questions. Also be prepared to answer questions about your unique experiences, such as military service, vocational training, membership on sports teams, and the like.

It is also important to be sure to get a good night's sleep before the interview and to eat sensibly (don't skip breakfast; don't stuff yourself at lunch) so that you can stay alert. Long interviews can be physically demanding.

Consider the interview an opportunity to ask questions as well as to answer them; most interviewers will give you an opportunity to ask whatever questions you'd like toward the end of an interview. Asking questions about an organization is a way to display enthusiasm for the job, as well as a means of assessing whether you really want to join the organization. You will want to know the following:

- Will there be any job training for this position?
- What are the opportunities for advancement?
- What is the atmosphere like in the work place? (You will also be able to observe this during the interview.)
- What hours do people work?
- Is there flexibility in scheduling the work day?
- When do you anticipate making a decision about this position?

The very first question you ask should *not* be, "How much does this job pay?" Usually the interviewer will discuss salary and benefits with you during the interview. If this is a preliminary interview and there is a chance you will be called back for another visit, you may want to defer questions about salary and benefits until you know that the organization is seriously considering you for the position.

During the interview, maintain eye contact and speak assertively. The goal in an interview is to project a positive attitude to the interviewer. As motivational speaker Zig Ziglar once noted, "Your attitude, not your aptitude, will determine your altitude."

TABLE A.1
Typical Questions Asked during a Job Interview[4]

I. Education

1. Why did you select your major area of study?
2. Why did you select your college/university?
3. If you were starting college again, what would you do differently? Why?
4. What subjects were most and least interesting? Useful? Why?
5. Other than the courses you studied, what is the most important thing you learned from your college experience?
6. How did you finance your college education?

II. Experience

7. What do you see as your strengths as an employee?
8. You say that a strength you have is _____. Give me some indication, perhaps an example, that illustrates this strength.
9. What special skills would you bring to this position?
10. Describe your last few work experiences. Why did you leave each one?
11. What were the best and worst aspects of your last job?
12. What were some of your achievements and disappointments in your last job?
13. Do you see yourself as a leader/manager of people? Why?
14. What kinds of work situations would you like to avoid? Why?
15. What frustrations have you encountered in your work experience? How have you handled these frustrations?
16. What do you look for in a boss?
17. Most employees and bosses have some disagreements. What are some things that you and your boss have disagreed about?

III. Position and Company

18. Why did you select this company?
19. Why did you decide to apply for this particular position?
20. How do you see yourself being qualified for this position?
21. Are you willing to relocate?

IV. Self-Evaluation

22. Tell me a little bit about yourself. Describe yourself.
23. What do you see as your personal strengths? Talents? How do you know that you possess these? Give examples of each.
24. What do you see as your weak points? Areas for improvement? Things you have difficulty doing? What have you done to deal with these?
25. Describe a specific work problem you had. Tell what you did to solve this problem.
26. What do you consider to be your greatest work achievement? Why?

V. Goals

27. Where do you see yourself being in your profession in five years? In ten years? How did you establish these goals? What will you need to do to achieve these goals?
28. What are your salary expectations for this position? Starting salary? Salary in five years?

Technology *and* Communication

Tips for E-Resumés

An **e-resumé is a resumé that is submitted in an electronic form via the Internet.** Given the dramatic growth in the number and popularity of e-resumés, chances are that you will send an e-resumé to a prospective employer rather than mailing or hand-delivering a "hard copy."[5] An e-resumé has several advantages:

- You can send your resumé to many people in a short amount of time.
- You can easily customize your resumé for different prospective employers, emphasizing the particular skills that the employer is seeking.
- You can showcase your computer and graphic skills if the job you are applying for requires those skills.[6]

When you develop your e-resumé, you have some decisions to make. First, do you use a "plain text" file, which does not permit you to enhance your resumé with formatting such as boldface, italics, or underlining but only uses unadorned words to sell your credentials? A plain text file is also called an ASCII file. It has the advantage of being easily distributed to many employers but it can be viewed by anyone, including your current employer whom you may not want to know that you are job hunting.[7] If you use an HTML resumé, which is basically a Web page, you can provide more formatting information and direct your resumé to a specific person or organization. Most consultants recommend an HTML format.[8]

Another decision to make is how widely you should distribute your e-resumé. Because it only takes a click of a mouse to send your resumé, you may be tempted to submit it to prospective employers whose job offerings are not quite a match for your skills. Resist this temptation. Because of the ease of submitting e-resumés, employers have been inundated with them, making it a challenge to sort through all of the resumés they receive. As in any communication situation, be audience centered. Send your resumé only to those you think are interested in someone with your credentials.

Most employers won't take the time to read attachments that you send along with your resumé. Rather than using attachments to your resumé to showcase work that you've done in the past, many experts recommend that you use a hyperlink to lead the e-resumé reader to your work samples. **A hyperlink is simply a connector between one page and another on the World Wide Web.**[9]

Although e-resumés have many advantages, you may still want to follow up with more personal approaches to the job search. Some employers specifically state that they do not want calls or visits, but unless you are prohibited from making follow-up contacts, it can be helpful to support your e-contact with a personal contact between you and your prospective employer.

Follow Up after the Interview

After the interview, it is wise to write a brief letter to thank the interviewer and to provide any additional information that he or she requested. You may also want to send a thank-you note to others in the organization, such as a secretary or administrative assistant, for helping you arrange the interview. If the interviewer asked for references, make sure you contact your references quickly and ask them to send letters of recommendation to the organization. Expedite this process by providing addressed, stamped envelopes and a copy of your resumé so that they can personalize their letters with specific information.

Is it appropriate to call the person who interviewed you to ask when a decision will be made about hiring someone? Some employers abide by the

Frank and Ernest

© Thaves. Reprinted with permission.

philosophy "Don't call us, we'll call you." But many others would interpret your call as a sign of your interest in the position and a testament to your ability to follow through. You may want to take the direct approach and simply ask your employer toward the end of the interview, "Would it be all right if I called you in a few days to see if you have made a decision or if you need additional information?" If the interviewer tells you a decision will be made by a certain date and that date passes by, it is probably okay to call and find out whether they've offered the job to someone else and to express your continued interest in the position if it hasn't been filled.

How to Be Interviewed in an Information-Gathering Interview

The bulk of the responsibility for an effective information-gathering interview falls on the shoulders of the person who is doing the interviewing. If you are the interviewer in an information-gathering interview, review the suggestions we offered earlier in this appendix for structuring the interview; most information-gathering interviews follow the general structure we outlined.

If you are the person being interviewed, however, your primary responsibilities are to be prepared, to listen carefully, and to respond appropriately to questions. In addition, a good interviewee knows what to expect in an information-gathering interview. You should prepare responses to anticipated questions, pay close attention to requests for specific information, and answer questions directly and accurately.

Prepare for the Interview

In most cases, interviewees have some advance knowledge of the purpose and objective of interviews, especially if someone is seeking specific information or advice. You can therefore anticipate probable topics of discussion. If you are uncertain what the interview is about, it is appropriate to ask the person who will interview you how to best prepare for the questions he or she plans to ask

On the Web

you. Yes, sometimes news programs have an interviewer pop up in an office, thrust a microphone in an interviewee's face, and ask a pointed question; in most cases, however, Mike Wallace of *60 Minutes* fame (or his equivalent) is not going to ambush you.

Depending on the nature of the interview, you may want to brush up on the facts you may be asked about. Jot down a few notes to remind you of names, dates, and places. In some cases, you may want to do some background reading on the topic of the interview.

Finally, think about not only what you will say in the interview but how you will respond nonverbally. Be on time. Maintain an attitude of interest and attentiveness with eye contact, attentive body positions, alert facial expressions, and an appropriately firm handshake.

Listen Effectively

Listen and Respond

Interviewing situations require you to listen to determine the amount and depth of information desired. If your responses are to be appropriate and useful, you must know what is being requested. If questions are unclear, ask for clarification or elaboration. By doing so, you can respond more fully and relevantly.

Successful interviewees also practice empathy. Interviewers are people, and interviewing situations are interpersonal encounters. Effective interviewees consider situations from interviewers' points of view, listen "between the lines" of what someone says to focus on underlying emotions, and watch for nonverbal cues. When interviewees listen to all facets of the communication, they can better adapt to the situation.

Respond Appropriately

Verbal

Just as questioning is the primary responsibility of an interviewer, responding is the primary responsibility of an interviewee. Keep answers direct, honest, and appropriate in depth and relevance. For example, in response to the question "How would you describe the quality of your relationship with your family?" don't give a 15-minute speech about your problems with your ex-spouse, keeping the children in clothes, and finding dependable home care for your aging parents. To make sure that you give the best possible answer, listen carefully when a question is posed and, if necessary, take a few moments to think before you answer. A response that is well thought out, straightforward, and relevant will be much more appreciated than one that is hasty, evasive, and unrelated to the question.

Using language and vocabulary appropriate to the situation is also important. The use of too much slang or technical terminology in an attempt to impress an interviewer can easily backfire by distracting the interviewer or distorting communication. Direct and simple language promotes understanding.

Finally, be adaptable and flexible to the needs of the interviewing situation. Some interviewers will ask questions to throw you off guard. When this happens, take a moment to think before you respond. Try to discover the reason for the question and respond to the best of your ability. Listen carefully for content *and* intent of questions so that you provide the information requested, especially when the interviewer changes topics. Flexibility and adaptability depend on good listening, empathy, accurate reading and interpretation of nonverbal communication, and practice. Just remember, "engage brain before opening mouth."

Adapt

The Responsibilities of the Interviewer

So far we've emphasized how to behave when you are the person being interviewed. As you assume leadership positions in your profession and community, you will undoubtedly be called on to interview others. In addition to knowing how to structure the opening, body, and conclusion of an interview, which we discussed earlier, there are several other characteristics of effective interviewers, whether you are seeking a future employee or simply gathering information.

Be Aware of Biases and Prejudices

First and foremost, an interviewer must be aware of his or her own biases and prejudices. Each person has a set of experiences, beliefs, attitudes, and values that influence how that person receives, interprets, and evaluates incoming stimuli. If accurate and useful information is to be shared in an interview, an interviewer must be aware of his or her own perceptual processes in order to make accurate and objective interpretations. An otherwise qualified candidate for a job shouldn't be eliminated from consideration just because the interviewer has a bias against redheads, for example.

Adapt to an Interviewee's Behavior

Skilled interviewers observe, evaluate, and adapt to the communication behavior of their interviewees. Because no two interviews—and no two interviewees—are exactly alike, interviewers adapt their communication behavior accordingly. A flexible communication style is a necessity. Interviewers should have predetermined plans, but they should not be thrown off balance if an interviewee suddenly turns the tables and asks, "How much money do *you* make for *your* job?"

Adaptability also includes the use of appropriate language and vocabulary. You should consciously choose language and vocabulary that interviewees will

Adapt

Knowing how to conduct an effective interview will help you determine if an applicant will be right for the job.

understand. Little is gained by the use of technical, ambiguous, or vague terms. Words should be straightforward, simple, and specific, but not so simple that interviewees feel "talked down" to. Empathy is important in determining the most appropriate language and vocabulary.

Deal Wisely with Sensitive Content

Verbal

When planning questions for an interview, consider possible sensitive topics and topics to be avoided. A question such as "Why were you fired from your last job?" will provoke a defensive reaction in a grievance interview.

   Good judgment and choice of words play crucial roles. One ill-chosen question can destroy the positive and open communication developed in an opening. Effective interviewers avoid potentially troublesome topics and attempt to put interviewees at ease. They discuss sensitive issues *if and only if* they are related to the purpose of the interviews. When a sensitive subject must be discussed, experienced interviewers choose their words carefully; thus, the question "Why were you fired?" might be rephrased as "How would you describe your relationship with your previous supervisor?"

Listen Effectively

Listen and Respond

The admonition to listen effectively has appeared frequently in this appendix. Effective listening is at the heart of any interview. No matter how well interviewers have prepared, the time will have been wasted if they are poor listeners. They need strong listening skills to make sure that they are receiving the kind and amount of information they need. They must be able to identify partial or irrelevant responses.

Highly developed listening skills also increase the ability to accurately perceive and interpret unintentional messages and beliefs, attitudes, and values. Interviewers learn a great deal from nonverbal, as well as verbal, communication.

Record Information

The information accumulated from an interview is useless if it is not recorded completely and accurately. A partial or inaccurate report can lead to poor decisions and mistaken actions. Take appropriate, legible written notes. If you use a tape or digital recorder, ask in advance for permission to use it.

Ask Appropriate Questions

The success of most interviews will be determined by the quality of the questions asked during the conversation. Think of questions as "mental can openers" designed to reveal how the other person thinks and behaves. Earlier we discussed question types (open, closed, probing, and hypothetical) and question sequences (funnel, inverted funnel, and tunnel). Some of your questions should be planned. Other questions may evolve from the discussion. Famed TV interviewer Larry King suggests that the best questions during an interview emerge from simply listening to what the other person is saying and then probing or following up on information and ideas verbalized.

Verbal

If you are interviewing a job applicant, you should be aware that there are certain questions that you should *not* ask. These are questions that are inappropriate because they ask for information that either laws or court interpretations of laws suggest could lead to illegal discrimination. Here's a list of topics you should not bring up during an employment interview when you're asking the questions.[10]

arrest records
less-than-honorable discharges
gender and marital status
maiden name
number of children
ages of children
number of preschool children
spouse's name
spouse's education
spouse's income
form of birth control
family plans
child care arrangements
car accidents
lawsuits
legal complaints
ownership of home
rental status

length of residence
date of high school graduation
age
sexual orientation
insurance claims
judgments
citizenship or national origin
mother's maiden name
place of birth
disabilities
handicap
illnesses or accidents
hospitalizations
current or prior
    medication/treatment
workers' compensation claims
weight
religion

church affiliation
social organizations
loans
wage assignments or
    garnishments

bankruptcy
credit cards
form of transportation
ownership of car

PRINCIPLES FOR A LIFETIME: Enhancing Your Skills

Principle One: Be aware of your communication with yourself and others.

Aware

- Take inventory of your skills and abilities to help you determine the job opportunities and careers that are best for you.
- Use your analysis of your talents to help you develop your resumé.
- During an interview, monitor your messages to ensure you are communicating clearly and effectively.

Principle Two: Effectively use and interpret verbal messages.

Verbal

- Speak clearly and respond to each question you are asked during an interview.
- Use action-oriented words on your resumé and during an interview to describe your accomplishments.
- Organize your resumé to include key elements of your education, experience, and special qualifications.
- Don't ask illegal or unethical questions during an employment interview.

Principle Three: Effectively use and interpret nonverbal messages.

Nonverbal

- Pay special attention to your appearance when you interview for a job; dress conservatively and appear neat and well groomed.
- Speak with confidence, use appropriate eye contact, and communicate interest and enthusiasm during the interview.
- When you interview someone, monitor your interviewee's nonverbal messages for clues about the individual's personality and ability to work with people.
- Skilled interviewers observe, evaluate, and then appropriately adapt to the communication behavior of interviewees.

Principle Four: Listen and respond thoughtfully to others.

Listen and Respond

- When you are interviewed for a job, be sure to stop, look, and listen to the questions and comments of the interviewer.
- Listen for both the details of the message and the major points or key ideas.
- When interviewing others, among your most important tasks is to listen.

Principle Five: Appropriately adapt messages to others.

Adapt

- Learn as much as you can about any prospective employer so that you can describe how your abilities best fit with the needs of the organization to which you are applying.

SUMMARY

An interview is a form of oral interaction structured to achieve a goal and involving two or more people who take turns speaking and listening. In this appendix, we have focused on tips and strategies for being interviewed and offered strategies for interviewing others. The five types of interview situations we've identified include the information-gathering interview, the appraisal interview, the problem-solving interview, the persuasion interview, and the job interview. This appendix focused primarily on job interviews and information-gathering interviews.

All interviews have an opening, in which the interviewee is put at ease; a body, during which questions are asked and answered; and a conclusion, which brings the interview to a comfortable close.

When you are seeking employment, start by becoming aware of your skills and abilities, and use your personal inventory to help you develop a well-written resumé. Focus on the needs of your prospective employer: Research the organization to which you are applying for a job. During the interview, listen carefully to the questions asked by the interviewer and respond appropriately. After the interview, it may be appropriate to send a thank-you note to the interviewer.

When preparing to be interviewed for an information-gathering interview, remember three primary tasks. First, prepare for the interview by reviewing information you think the interviewer will ask you about. Second, listen closely to the questions that you are being asked. Finally, respond appropriately by keeping answers direct and honest. Don't ramble. Observe the nonverbal responses of the interviewer to determine whether you are appropriately answering the questions.

We concluded this appendix by summarizing the essential requirements when you interview others. Don't let your own biases and prejudices interfere with your job of listening and responding to the interviewee. Although it's useful to have a prepared list of questions to ask, be prepared to adapt to the interviewee's behavior. The best interviews have a spontaneous flow rather than a rigid structure. Don't ask illegal questions during a job interview, and handle sensitive questions with tact and diplomacy. Listening well is the hallmark of an effective interviewer. Develop a strategy to record the information you gather from the interview. Finally, the key to any interview is the quality of the questions asked. As the interviewer, you have prime responsibility for asking clear, appropriate, and answerable questions.

Technology and Interpersonal Communication

APPENDIX OBJECTIVES

After studying this appendix, you should be able to

1. Discuss ways that technological innovations
   have affected the formation and development
   of interpersonal relationships.

2. Describe the role of technology in
   relationship maintenance.

W hat happens when the power goes out? Probably all of us have been in a severe storm or other circumstance that caused our electric service to be disrupted. Were you prepared—meaning did you have candles or flashlights on hand? Had you saved whatever you were doing on your computer before you lost power? Did you have a battery-operated radio so that you could get weather updates? Or did you just sleep through the whole thing?

At times like these, when severe storms or other problems cause a power outage, we realize how pervasively technology (and the electricity that powers most of it) affects our lives. We realize the need for such simple things as batteries, flashlights and matches, canned food and a manual can opener, and a regular or cell phone (instead of a cordless one that has to be plugged into a socket to function). We may also wish we knew the names of our neighbors.

Many people are concerned about the world's seeming obsession with technology, because it seems that we become enamored with the technology before we stop to think: Is this really the best thing for my life? for my relationships with other people? for society? for future generations?[1]

No one doubts the wonders of technology and the many ways in which technological advances have improved everyday life. We have almost stopped marveling at how quickly a meal can be prepared, a document can be written and edited, and a message can travel around the world. We can be exposed to and learn about other cultures around the globe, so technology helps us embrace diversity. In this appendix we explore some positive effects of technology on interpersonal relationships. But we also pause to consider the effect of "instant everything" on our relationships and communication with other people. Our main point is this: Technology is part of modern life in much of the world, and technological advances will keep on coming. But before we become completely dazzled by the next innovation, we should apply our critical thinking powers to consider whether the innovation is positive or negative, healthy or harmful for our lives, our relationships, and the culture in which we function. Is technology bringing people together or pulling them apart? Does technology make communication with others easier and faster or more difficult and time-consuming?

An Impersonal Technological Innovation

When was the last time you called a government agency, a utility company, or a bank and a real, live human being answered the phone? Most often, we hear something like this: "Welcome to _____'s automated customer service system. This call is being monitored so that we can improve our service. Please listen to the following menu of items before selecting an option. For _____, press 1; for _____, press 2," and so forth. Then, when you make your selection from the opening menu, you'll likely hear something like this: "Thank you for your selection. For current account information, press 1; for inquiries about _____, press 2"—another set of menu options. The very last option, if it's an option at all, is usually, "To speak to a service representative, please stay on the line and your call will be answered in the order it was received." You can grow old on that line.

If this sounds painfully familiar, then you have probably already wondered whether this technological advance is a good thing or not. **An interactive voice response, a recorded menu of options that callers encounter in many phone systems,** reduces labor costs and may allow customers 24-hour access to information. However, market research shows that when customers encounter this technology, their satisfaction decreases in proportion to the length of the list of menu choices.[2] Some of you reading this are too young to know this, but many of us remember a time when you could dial a company (dial, rather than push buttons on a telephone) and actually speak to someone. Perhaps things were slower and less efficient then, but it did seem somehow more personal, even more enjoyable to have a real person attend to your concerns.

Enter technological innovation: **the chatterbot, a robot in the form of a computer software program that simulates a human voice and can respond to questions placed by online users.** In a newspaper article describing this device, a journalist begins by explaining, "People find Alice easy to talk to. She listens more than she speaks. She says she likes dining by candlelight. She reads newspapers and news magazines, so she is up on popular culture. But Alice's favorite topic of conversation is robots. That's because she is one."[3] Reading further, we discover that Alice (full name: Artificial Linguistic Computer Entity) is a computer software program that simulates conversations with humans. Chatterbots are being developed to act as customer service representatives, information deliverers, and even "potential companions for human surfers in the sometimes lonely world of the Web."[4] A person asks a question of a chatterbot, which searches for word clues in the question and matches them to its vast database of English words. It then attempts to offer a helpful response, even a personalized one by inserting the name of the questioner into the response. Chatterbots are but one form of artificial intelligence that attempts to make machines operate like people.

"On the Internet, nobody knows you're a dog."

What are the pros and cons of such a device? On the pro side, we can see an advantage to having a human-like response to a question instead of a recording, words on a computer screen, or dead air. The news article gives as an example someone entering an online music store, conversing with a chatterbot about musical tastes, and receiving the chatterbot's recommendations for artists the consumer may not have heard of. But just like the menu approach to customer service calls, chatterbots simply can't deal with some questions or concerns. Chatterbots may also give those "lonely surfers" described in the article a false sense of a social connection—a feeling that a human-to-human conversation has occurred when it actually has not. What about the ethics involved? What if someone thinks she or he is chatting with a person (perhaps named Alice), but instead is chatting with a machine? In computer applications, such programs are clearly identified as artificial intelligence or human simulation devices, but it's possible such devices could be used by the unscrupulous to dupe the public.

One of the most obvious technological advances to affect human relationships is the ability to communicate in cyberspace. Just what is cyberspace? One interesting description of *cyberspace* is "the diverse experiences of space associated with computing and related technologies."[5] Most of us who communicate in cyberspace do so through that technological marvel known as the Internet. The Internet has become an invaluable tool for accomplishing a variety of tasks—e-mailing, instant messaging, downloading music, conducting research, and buying products and services. Estimates indicate that over 600 million people worldwide use these types of Internet services, and that yearly business transactions conducted online number in the trillions. Research has determined that 72% of Americans go online at least once a month. A fairly recent development that is gaining popularity is "blogging," short for Web logging—live journaling on the Internet. Many Web sites include blogging spaces now, which offer forums for free expression to all visitors to the site. Over 500,000 people are estimated to be active "bloggers."[6] In the next few pages, we explore online tools for initiating relationships and connecting people; then we discuss the role of computer-mediated communication in ongoing relationships.

The Role of Technology in Relationship Initiation

In Chapter 2.1 we discussed interpersonal communication and the initiation of relationships. How has technology helped and hurt these processes? First, our Principle One, of being aware of your communication with yourself and others, is affected by technology. We've described how important it is to know yourself, to develop your self-concept and monitor what affects your self-esteem as you form relationships—friendships, dating or romantic relationships, and workplace connections. But what about relationships that develop only in cyberspace? Do cyber-relationships have as much potential impact on one's self-concept as other relationships?

One of the more interesting opportunities that Internet relationships afford is the ability to alter and expand one's identity.[7] Some researchers describe identity in the virtual world as "fluid," meaning that we don't really know who we're chatting with online, who their families are, where they're located, and so forth. Our chatting partners don't know much about us either. In such a virtual world, power and status are equalized and minimized, but the potential for deception is expanded.[8] We're not advocating that you deceive people when chatting online or e-mailing, because that's unethical. It can also lead to potential abuse and disastrous consequences, as evidenced in stories about young children who pretend to be adults online and form connections with highly disturbed people, such as sexual predators. But apart from these extreme cases, the opportunity exists to experiment with your identity online and note the response you get from others. You can test untapped parts of your personality, perhaps by being more bold or more sensitive than you normally are in your face-to-face relationships. You can expand who you are and adjust who you want to become based on others' reactions.

We're all probably aware of the increase in people's use of verbal communication skills (Principle Two) to make connections with others via the Internet. Online users can communicate in **synchronous time, meaning that there is little to no lag time between comments.** Such Internet tools as IRC (Internet Relay Chat) allow users to read and respond to others' comments on a computer screen as the remarks are being generated. It's as close to in-person chatting in real time as is possible on a computer, given the current tech-

Verbal

This Marine Corps medic uses his blog "Doc in the Box" to communicate vital information about members of his unit.

nology. In recent years, instant messaging, sometimes in the form of text messaging via cell phones or personal computers, has become an increasingly popular method of communicating, especially among teens and young adults. Devices such as Blackberries and PDAs (personal data assistants), which offer a combination of services such as cell phone and e-mail options, are extremely popular and are becoming more affordable. However, there can be a downside to the use of such technology: Blackberries are occasionally referred to as "crackberries" because they can become addictive for users. The temptation to use one's instant messaging device during class or work hours can be irresistible, but doing so creates a distraction. Another negative result of the use of such devices may be that more communication occurs through computer-mediated channels than face to face.[9] Others prefer to converse in **asynchronous time, meaning that online messages posted at one time are read at another time.** Asynchronous communication among online users who are interested in a common topic or who belong to a specific organization may take place through **a newsgroup, in which postings by subscribers go out to all members, who then can respond with their own postings.** However, involvement in newsgroups, which is one of the oldest components of the Internet, dating back to 1979, has seriously declined. The decline is primarily related to *spam* (electronic garbage or junk mail) and to spammers' increasingly sophisticated means of disguising themselves as newsgroup subscribers, all the while clogging newsgroups as they hawk their products and services.[10] Similar to the newsgroup is **the listserv, which involves a "host" and software that facilitates discussions by linking people who share common interests.**[11] Yet another option is **the electronic bulletin board, which anyone, not just a subscriber, can access and read postings on**.[12]

Perhaps you've made friendships with people you've never met in person, and these virtual friendships have become just as valuable as your face-to-face friendships. You may even be one of those brave souls who has made a "love connection" over the Internet.[13] Online dating services such as Yahoo personals, Match.com, and eharmony.com have experienced record success in recent years. While online dating may have once been seen as a refuge for social misfits, it is now a booming business, as sites have improved security measures and as more romantic "success stories" receive publicity.[14] One study found that relationships established online were just as satisfying to the partners participating in the study as those that were established the "old-fashioned way" through nonmediated channels.[15]

What makes virtual relationships attractive? Many users enjoy the freedom of getting to know other people without some of the nonverbal dimensions that give us pause in face-to-face interaction, primarily the dimension of physical attractiveness.[16] As Annette Markham explains in her fascinating book *Life Online: Researching Real Experience in Virtual Space,* some people feel trapped by their offline selves—both their bodies and the roles they play. As their online selves, they can transcend the trappings of physicality. One user Markham interviewed in her research felt that her appearance was a hindrance when she met people face to face. She was much more confident of her ability to connect with people through her use of language because, as the user put it, "eloquence makes me beautiful online."[17]

Nonverbal

A second reason people are drawn to electronic communication as a means of establishing relationships relates to the ability to edit one's messages—a form of adaptation (Principle Five) not easily managed in face-to-face communication. In Chapter 1.3 on verbal communication, we discussed something most of us have experienced—saying the wrong thing to someone and then trying to take it back or undo the damage we've caused. In such instances we wish we could have a chance to change our inane or hurtful comment. Electronic communication provides this editing opportunity, unless you hit "enter" too quickly.

Verbal
Adapt

Another aspect of cyber-relating that is attractive, but also disturbing to many people (particularly people in committed, monogamous relationships), is the potential to stray from one's committed partner by making virtual connections. This trend has called into question the concept of fidelity; it's hard to determine if developing emotionally intimate relationships online with someone other than one's partner is a form of cheating.[18] Many believe that there is a clear difference between establishing emotionally supportive relationships online and developing sexual relationships online. But might both be considered a breach of faith by one's partner?

Robert Weiss, Director of the Sexual Recovery Institute of Los Angeles, remarked, "This [Internet usage] totally reinvents adultery. If you have a totally cyber-sexual intimacy with someone you've never met, have you had an affair?"[19] While some believe online flirtations are harmless, like office flirtations that don't escalate into romantic relationships or affairs, others see online relationships as outgrowths of a problem within the primary relationship. Energy that once might have been directed toward the primary relationship now becomes directed to virtual relationships.

The Role of Technology in Relationship Maintenance

One of the most obvious positive uses of electronic communication is the ability to keep up with people who live long distances from us. E-mail, instant messaging, and online chatting are more economical ways to maintain relationships than carrying on long-distance telephone conversations or traveling to be together. For many people, online communication doesn't replace the good old personal letter delivered via "snail mail," but it is much faster and more immediate, in that you can transmit what you're thinking and get a rapid response. Some online users develop **virtual communities, like MUDs (Multi-User Dimensions or Dungeons) or MOOs (MUD Object Oriented), for such purposes as generating political activism, exploring common interests, collaborating on projects, and socializing.**[20] According to MUD users, these virtual communities can be just as supportive and sustaining as any in-person community established on campus or in a neighborhood.[21] So, in a sense, technology has brought us closer together as a nation and a world, because we can communicate quickly, regularly, and economically across great distances.

However, some argue that electronic communication, among other forms of technological innovation, actually pulls people apart more than it brings them together. According to this view, something is wrong when we converse regularly across the world with people we're not likely to meet but do not know or socialize with our neighbors down the hall or across the street. Some people rely too heavily on e-mail because it lets them avoid nerve-wracking or uncomfortable in-person conversation.[22]

The question is, which community is more "real"—the in-person one or the virtual one? Electronic communication can create a false sense of community, because computer users who interact across the globe most often do so alone, in the small spaces of their private existences. Likewise, the rising popularity of the home office connected to a virtual world has the potential to diminish the social or communal impact of the workplace.[23]

Many people actually prefer computer-mediated intimacy to in-person intimacy. Some prefer it to the point of becoming **cyber-addicts, meaning that they spend all of their free time surfing the Net and making online connections. Some cyber-addicts jeopardize their jobs or school performance because they spend so much time online.** The Sexual Recovery Institute published a checklist to help people determine if they or someone they know has reached the stage of cyber-addiction. Some warning signs include (1) spending increasing amounts of online time focused on sexual or romantic intrigue or involvement; (2) not considering online sexual or romantic affairs to be a possible violation of one's commitment to one's spouse or partner; (3) online use interfering with work, in that the user is tired or late to work because of the previous night's use; and (4) online use interfering with primary relationships, because users minimize or lie to partners about online activities and spend less time with family or partners.[24]

Listen and Respond

As a communication channel, e-mail is better for some relationships than others. It's a great way to communicate information, check perceptions, and stay in touch with busy colleagues and friends, both near and far. But close or intimate relationships—family relationships, friendships, and romantic relationships—typically require more than just e-mail to maintain closeness. E-mail is also better for some topics than others. In close relationships, e-mail tends to work best for quick updates or brief expressions of affection and to make plans or share ideas. The reply function in e-mail software serves our Principle Four, that of listening and responding. Once you've read an e-mail message, the most expedient thing to do is to use the reply function and generate an immediate response. But what about self-disclosure, communication described in Chapter 2.1 as critical to the development of trust and intimacy in relationships? Self-disclosing in an electronic format has pros and cons. On the pro side: In some circumstances you might decide to electronically share information that you deem safe—meaning that it isn't too personal but it is still self-disclosure. Some research shows that self-disclosure occurs earlier and is more intimate between persons developing their relationship online than between those developing their relationship through more conventional methods. The difference mostly relates to anonymity. Since anonymity is possible in computer-mediated relationships, participants feel more free to disclose about themselves. In contrast, the lack of anonymity in face-to-face encounters can create psychological discomfort and a need to protect oneself. Thus, face-to-face self-disclosure often develops more slowly and requires repeated exposure to one's partner and a gradual increase in trust.[25] Perhaps the best aspect of electronic self-disclosure is its potential effect on reciprocity. While the recipient of your electronic disclosure might choose not to reply quickly and in kind, the technology makes it easy to reciprocate if he or she so desires.

On the con side, remember that e-mail messages generated at work or school aren't your private property. Be careful what you disclose online, because people other than the person you intend to receive the message could learn this information about you. There are computer programs that will keep e-mail generated from one's personal computer completely private, meaning that once a message has been sent and read, it can be completely erased from a computer's memory and hard drive. However, most of us don't own such a program. So even a deleted message can be retrieved by an expert or hacker.

Self-disclosure may also work better when communicated in person because of the tendency for the discloser to feel vulnerable. Although some avid online users disagree, face-to-face communication involves more channels of information than e-mail. In face-to-face encounters we call on all our verbal and nonverbal communication skills to self-disclose to another person in an appropriate manner.[26] We also need to be able to see and hear the other person's reactions to our disclosure—verbal and nonverbal—to determine the effects on our relationship. In Chapter 1.4 we provided a list of "emoticons," symbols people often use to convey emotions or to add a more human expression to their e-mail messages. But these can only go so far; they are generally ineffective when personal information and serious emotions are involved.

Verbal
Nonverbal

This information relates to our Principle Five, adaptation, because it's important to learn to adapt your message to your receivers, but also to adapt by selecting the most appropriate channel for communication. One suggestion particularly relevant to our discussion is this: Never communicate anything electronically that you would not say in person. If you would have trouble conveying something in person, don't fall prey to the false sense of anonymity or face-saving attributes of e-mail to bail you out of a difficult conversation.[27] Think long and hard about which channel of communication you should use for certain kinds of information and in certain relationships. First consider what the relationship means to you; then put yourself in your relational partner's shoes and think about the way you'd prefer to receive the information.

Adapt

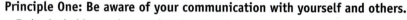

PRINCIPLES FOR A LIFETIME: Enhancing Your Skills

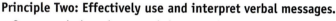

Principle One: Be aware of your communication with yourself and others.

Aware

- Technological innovations, such as Internet chat rooms, allow you to explore your identity and note the responses you get from other online users.

Principle Two: Effectively use and interpret verbal messages.

Verbal

- Some people have better verbal communication skills online than in face-to-face interaction.
- Edit electronic messages; don't say something in an e-mail message or as a comment in a chat room that you would not say to someone in person.
- Be careful when self-disclosing via an electronic channel; e-mail isn't necessarily private, and self-disclosure may be more effectively communicated in person.

Principle Three: Effectively use and interpret nonverbal messages.

Nonverbal

- Some people enjoy the freedom of getting to know people online, without the constraints of nonverbal dimensions, such as appearance and physical attractiveness.
- Be careful when self-disclosing over an electronic channel, because self-disclosure is more effectively accomplished when nonverbal cues accompany verbal ones.
- Emoticons are keyboard symbols that help convey nonverbal elements of an electronic message, such as tone of voice and emphasis.

Principle Four: Listen and respond thoughtfully to others.

Listen and Respond

- One advantage of e-mail and other forms of electronic communication is the potential for an immediate response; learn to use the reply function.

Principle Five: Appropriately adapt messages to others.

Adapt

- One advantage of electronic communication is the ability to edit your message and adapt it to receivers *before* you communicate it.
- Learn to adapt your message as well as the channel for your message. If you have bad news or negative information to relate to someone, in-person communication is preferable to electronic communication.

SUMMARY

Interpersonal relationships that form in cyberspace offer particular challenges. While you can experiment with your online identity and explore parts of your personality, there is the potential for unethical behavior in misrepresenting yourself to another online user. Relationships can form and be maintained via technology such as e-mail; however, for some forms of interpersonal communication and some relationships, cyber-channels are inappropriate. E-mail and other online channels of communication, such as electronic bulletin boards, listservs, and newsgroups, allow rapid communication with distant partners, but some scholars worry that these forms of technology are segmenting our culture, rather than uniting us.

Notes

INTRODUCTION

1. For an excellent review of intrapersonal communication theory and research, see D. Voate, *Intrapersonal Communication: Different Voices, Different Minds* (Hillsdale, NJ: Lawrence Erlbaum, 1994).
2. D. Quinn, *My Ishmael* (New York: Bantam Books, 1996).
3. L. Barker, R. Edwards, C. Gaines, K. Gladney, and F. Holley, "An Investigation of Proportional Time Spent in Various Communication Activities of College Students," *Journal of Applied Communication Research 8* (1981): 101–109.

CHAPTER 2.1

1. See S. B. Barnes, *Computer-Mediated Communication: Human-to-Human Communication across the Internet* (Boston: Pearson, 2003); L. C. Tidwell and J. B. Walther, "Computer-Mediated Communication Effects on Disclosure, Impressions, and Interpersonal Evaluations: Getting to Know One Another a Bit at a Time," *Human Communication Research 28* (2002): 317–348; J. B. Walther, C. L. Slovacek, and L. C. Tidwell, "Is a Picture Worth a Thousand Words? Photographic Images in Long-Term and Short-Term Computer-Mediated Communication," *Communication Research 28* (2001): 105–134; J. T. Hancock and P. J. Dunham, "Impression Formation in Computer-Mediated Communication Revisited: An Analysis of the Breadth and Intensity of Impressions," *Communication Research 28* (2001): 325–347.
2. K. M. Galvin and C. Wilkinson, "The Communication Process: Impersonal and Interpersonal." In *Making Connections: Readings in Relational Communication*, edited by K. M. Galvin and P. Cooper (Los Angeles, CA: Roxbury, 1996), 4–10; Y. Abraham, "Aspiring Doctors Have a New Exam to Pass: Bedside Manner 101," *Corpus Christi Caller Times* (July 20, 2003): A14.
3. E. Berscheid, "Interpersonal Attraction." In *The Handbook of Social Psychology*, edited by G. Lindzey and E. Aronson (New York: Random House, 1985), 413–484, as reported in J. A. Simpson and B. A. Harris, "Interpersonal Attraction." In *Perspectives on Close Relationships*, edited by A. L. Weber and J. H. Harvey (Boston: Allyn & Bacon, 1994), 45–66.
4. W. Stoebe, "Self-Esteem and Interpersonal Attraction." In *Theory and Practice in Interpersonal Attraction*, edited by S. Duck (London: Academic Press, 1977).
5. See D. T. Kenrick, S. L. Neuberg, and R. B. Cialdini, *Social Psychology: Unraveling the Mystery* 3e (Boston: Allyn & Bacon, 2004); L. K. Guerrero, P. A. Andersen, and W. A. Afifi, *Close Encounters: Communicating in Relationships* (New York: McGraw-Hill, 2001); E. Berscheid and H. T. Reis, "Attraction and Close Relationships." In *The Handbook of Social Psychology* 4e, Vol. 2, edited by D. T. Gilbert, S. T. Fiske, and G. Lindzey (New York: Oxford University Press, 1998), 193–281; V. Sharma and T. Kaur, "Interpersonal Attraction in Relation to Similarity and Help," *Psychological Studies 39* (1995): 84–87; T. Shaikh and S. Kanakar, "Attitudinal Similarity and Affiliation Need as Determinants of Interpersonal Attraction," *Journal of Social Psychology 134* (1994): 257–259; S. S. Brehm, R. Miller, D. Perlman, and S. M. Campbell, *Intimate Relationships* 3e (New York: McGraw-Hill, 2001); M. Sunnafrank, "Interpersonal Attraction and Attitude Similarity: A Communication-Based Assessment." In *Communication Yearbook 14*, edited by J. A. Andersen (Newbury Park, CA: Sage, 1991), 451–483; J. E. Lydon, D. W. Jamieson, and M. Zanna, "Interpersonal Similarity and the Social and Intellectual Dimensions of First Impressions," *Social Cognition 6* (1988): 269–286.
6. K. Y. A. McKenna, A. S. Green, and M. E. J. Gleason, "Relationship Formation on the Internet: What's the Big Attraction?" *Journal of Social Issues 58* (2002): 9–31.

7. B. R. Burleson, A. W. Kunkel, and J. D. Birch, "Thoughts about Talk in Romantic Relationships: Similarity Makes for Attraction (and Happiness, Too)," *Communication Quarterly 42* (1994): 259–273; A. E. Varnadore, S. C. Howe, and S. Brownlow, "Why Do I Like You? Students' Understanding of the Impact of the Factors That Contribute to Liking." Paper presented at the meeting of the Southeastern Psychological Association, March, 1994.

8. Sunnafrank, "Interpersonal Attraction and Attitude Similarity."

9. D. Garner, "Harmless Crushes Can Be Uplifting," *Corpus Christi Caller Times* (December 3, 1996): H1, H4.

10. J. H. Harvey and A. L. Weber, *Odyssey of the Heart: Close Relationships in the 21st Century* 2e (Mahwah, NJ: Lawrence Erlbaum, 2002); Kenrick et al., *Social Psychology*; M. L. Knapp and J. A. Hall, *Nonverbal Communication in Human Interaction* 5e (Belmont, CA: Wadsworth, 2002); M. Crawford and R. Unger, *Women and Gender: A Feminist Psychology* 4e (New York: McGraw-Hill, 2003).

11. A. Cooper and L. Sportolari, "Romance in Cyberspace: Understanding Online Attraction," *Journal of Sex Education and Therapy 22* (1997): 7–14; McKenna, "Relationship Formation on the Internet."

12. A. Cooper, I. P. McLoughlin, and K. M. Campbell, "Sexuality in Cyberspace: Update for the 21st Century," *Cyberpsychology & Behavior 32* (2000): 521–536.

13. Guerrero, *Close Encounters*, 59.

14. See A. Botta, "Television Images and Adolescent Girls' Body Image Disturbance," *Journal of Communication 49* (1999): 22–37; M. Wiederman and S. R. Hurst, "Body Size, Physical Attractiveness, and Body Image among Young Adult Women: Relationships to Sexual Experience and Sexual Esteem," *Journal of Sex Research 35* (1998): 272–281; L. Lazier and A. Gagnard Kendrick, "Women in Advertisements: Sizing Up the Images, Roles, and Functions." In *Women in Mass Communication* 2e, edited by P. Creedon (Newbury Park, CA: Sage, 1993), 199–219; A. Gagnard, "From Feast to Famine: Depiction of Ideal Body Type in Magazine Advertising: 1950–1984." In *Proceedings of the Nineteen Eighty-Six Conference of the American Academy of Advertising*, edited by E. F. Larkin (Charleston, SC: American Academy of Advertising, 1986), R46–R50; B. Silverstein, L. Perdue, B. Peterson, and E. Kelly, "The Role of Mass Media in Promoting a Thin Standard of Bodily Attractiveness for Women," *Sex Roles 14* (1986): 519–532.

15. S. W. Duck, *Personal Relationships and Personal Constructs: A Study of Friendship Formation* (New York: John Wiley & Sons, 1973).

16. E. H. Walster, V. Aronson, D. Abrahams, and L. Rottmann, "Importance of Physical Attractiveness in Dating Behavior," *Journal of Personality and Social Psychology 4* (1966): 508–516; V. B. Hinsz, "Facial Resemblance in Engaged and Married Couples," *Journal of Social and Personal Relationships 6* (1989): 223–229.

17. A. Feingold, "Gender Differences in Effects of Physical Attractiveness on Romantic Attraction: A Comparison across Five Research Paradigms," *Journal of Personality and Social Psychology 59* (1990): 981–993.

18. Guerrero, *Close Encounters*; Kenrick, *Social Psychology*; Knapp and Hall, *Nonverbal Communication in Human Interaction*.

19. K. R. Van Horn, A. Arnone, K. Nesbitt, L. Desilets, T. Sears, M. Giffin, and R. Brudi, "Physical Distance and Interpersonal Characteristics in College Students' Romantic Relationships," *Personal Relationships 4* (1997): 15–24; M. E. Rohlfing, "'Doesn't Anybody Stay in One Place Anymore?' An Exploration of the Understudied Phenomenon of Long-Distance Relationships." In *Understudied Relationships: Off the Beaten Track*, edited by J. T. Wood and S. Duck (Thousand Oaks, CA: Sage, 1995), 173–196; L. Stafford and J. R. Reske, "Idealization and Communication in Long-Distance Premarital Relationships," *Family Relations 39* (1990): 274–279; T. Stephen, "Communication and Interdependence in Geographically Separated Relationships," *Human Communication Research 13* (1986): 191–210.

20. Brehm, *Intimate Relationships*.

21. E. R. Merkle and R. A. Richardson, "Digital Dating and Virtual Relating: Conceptualizing Computer-Mediated Relationships," *Family Relations 49* (2000): 187–196.

22. <http://www.wildxangel.com>; <http://www.bol.ucla.edu>; <http://www.thirdage.com>; <http://www.onlinedatingmagazine.com>.

23. Guerrero, *Close Encounters*; Brehm, *Intimate Relationships*.

24. W. Schutz, *FIRO: A Three-Dimensional Theory of Interpersonal Behavior* (New York: Holt, Rinehart, and Winston, 1960).

25. A. Mehrabian, *Nonverbal Communication* (Chicago: Aldine-Atherton, 1972).

26. J. A. Daly, E. Hogg, D. Sacks, M. Smith, and L. Zimring, "Sex and Relationship Affect Social Self-Grooming." In *The Nonverbal Communication Reader: Classic and Contemporary Readings* 2e, edited by L. K. Guerrero, J. DeVito, and M. L. Hecht (Prospect Heights, IL: Waveland, 1999), 56–61.

27. M. T. Whitty, "Cyber-Flirting: An Examination of Men's and Women's Flirting Behaviour Both Offline and on the Internet," *Behaviour Change 21* (2004): 115–126.

28. Merkel and Richardson, "Digital Dating and Virtual Relating," 190.

29. For research on initial interaction in online relationships, see A. Ramirez, Jr. and J. K. Burgoon, "The Effect of Interactivity on Initial Interactions: The Influence of Information Valence and Modality and Information Richness on Computer-Mediated Interaction," *Communication Monographs 71* (2004): 422–447; J. B. Walther and M. R. Parks, "Cues Filtered out, Cues Filtered in: Computer-Mediated Communication and Relationships." In *Handbook of Interpersonal Communication* 3e, edited by M. L. Knapp and J. A. Daly (Thousand Oaks, CA: Sage, 2002), 529–563; J. A. McCown, D. Fischer, R. Page, and M. Homant, "Internet Relationships: People Who Meet People," *Cyberpsychology & Behavior 4* (2001): 593–596; McKenna, "Relationship Formation on the Internet."

30. C. R. Berger and R. J. Calabrese, "Some Explorations in Initial Interaction and Beyond: Toward a Developmental Theory of Interpersonal Communication," *Human Communication Research 1* (1975): 99–112; C. R. Berger and J. J. Bradac, *Language and Social Knowledge: Uncertainty in Interpersonal Relations* (Baltimore: Edward Arnold, 1982).

31. McCown, "Internet Relationships."

32. McKenna, "Relationship Formation on the Internet."

33. Merkle and Richardson, "Digital Dating and Virtual Relating," 191.

34. A. N. Joinson and B. Dietz-Uhler, "Explanations for the Perpetration of and Reactions to Deception in a Virtual Community," *Social Science Computer Review 20* (2002): 275–289; D. Knox, V. Daniels, L. Sturdivant, and M. E. Zusman, "College Student Use of the Internet for Mate Selection," *College Student Journal 35* (2001): 158–160; McCown, "Internet Relationships."

35. C. L. Kleinke, F. B. Meeker, and R. A. Staneski, "Preference for Opening Lines: Comparing Ratings by Men and Women," *Sex Roles 15* (1986): 585–600.

36. E. Weber, *How to Pick Up Girls!* (New York: Bantam Books, 1970).

37. For research on sex roles and interaction, see P. A. Mongeau, M. C. M. Serewicz, and L. F. Therrien, "Goals for Cross-Sex First Dates: Identification, Measurement, and the Influence of Contextual Factors," *Communication Monographs 71* (2004): 121–147; C. L. Clark, P. R. Shaver, and M. F. Abrahams, "Strategic Behaviors in Romantic Relationship Initiation," *Personality and Social Psychology Bulletin 25* (1999): 707–720; A. E. Lindsey and W. R. Zakahi, "Perceptions of Men and Women Departing from Conversational Sex Role Stereotypes during Initial Interaction." In *Sex Differences and Similarities in Communication*, edited by D. J. Canary and K. Dindia (Mahwah, NJ: Lawrence Erlbaum, 1998), 393–412; A. E. Lindsey and W. R. Zakahi, "Women Who Tell and Men Who Ask: Perceptions of Men and Women Departing from Gender Stereotypes during Initial Interaction," *Sex Roles 34* (1996): 767–786; L. A. McCloskey, "Gender and Conversation: Mixing and Matching Styles." In *Current Conceptions of Sex Roles and Sex Typing: Theory and Research*, edited by D. B. Carter (New York: Praeger, 1987), 139–153; J. Coates, *Women, Men, and Language* 3e (New York: Pearson, 2004); V. Derlega, B. Winstead, P. Wong, and S. Hunter, "Gender Effects in an Initial Encounter: A Case Where Men Exceeded Women in Disclosure," *Journal of Social and Personal Relationships 2* (1985): 25–44; R. Lakoff, *Language and Woman's Place* (New York: Harper & Row, 1975); P. M. Fishman, "Interaction: The Work Women Do," *Social Problems 25* (1978): 397–406; J. D. Davis, "When Boy Meets Girl: Sex Roles and the Negotiation of Intimacy in an Acquaintance Exercise," *Journal of Personality and Social Psychology 36* (1978): 684–692.

38. A. L. Vangelisti, M. L. Knapp, and J. A. Daly, "Conversational Narcissism," *Communication Monographs 57* (1990): 251–274.

39. C. Derber, *The Pursuit of Attention: Power and Ego in Everyday Life* (New York: Oxford University Press, 2000).

40. J. Holmes, "Complimenting—A Positive Politeness Strategy." In *Language and Gender: A Reader*, edited by J. Coates (Malden, MA: Blackwell, 1998), 100–120.

41. E. M. Doohan and V. Manusov, "The Communication of Compliments in Romantic Relationships: An Investigation of Relational Satisfaction and Sex Differences and Similarities in Compliment Behavior," *Western Journal of Communication 68* (2004): 170–194.

42. S. Jourard, *The Transparent Self* (Princeton, NJ: Van Nostrand, 1971); J. C. Pearson, *Interpersonal Communication: Concepts, Components, and Contexts* 2e (New York: McGraw-Hill, 1990).

43. Harvey and Weber, *Odyssey of the Heart*, 105–106.

44. S. Petronio, "The Boundaries of Privacy: Praxis of Everyday Life." In *Balancing Secrets of Private Disclosure*, edited by S. Petronio (Mahwah, NJ: Lawrence Erlbaum, 2000), 37–49; L. B. Rosenfeld, "Overview of the Ways Privacy, Secrecy, and Disclosure Are Balanced in Today's Society." In Petronio, *Balancing Secrets of Private Disclosure*, 3–17; C. A. Wilkinson, "Expressing Affection: A Vocabulary of Loving Messages." In Galvin and Cooper, *Making Connections*, 150–157; Guerrero, *Close Encounters.*

45. M. L. Rasmussen, "The Problem of Coming Out," *Theory into Practice 43* (2004): 144–151; T. W. Harrison, "Adolescent Homosexuality and Concerns Regarding Disclosure," *Journal of School Health 73* (2003): 107–119; R. Galatzer and B. J. Cohler, "Making a Gay Identity: Coming Out, Social Context, and Psychodynamics," *Annual of Psychoanalysis 30* (2002): 256–286.

46. C. A. Vanlear, Jr., "The Formation of Social Relationships: A Longitudinal Study of Social Penetration," *Human Communication Research 13* (1987): 299–322.

47. Harvey and Weber, *Odyssey of the Heart.*

48. J. Fine, "Intimacy," *O: The Oprah Winfrey Magazine* (October, 2001), 225.

49. For research on the role of self-disclosure in relationship development, see M. Kito, "Self-Disclosure in Romantic Relationships and Friendships Among American and Japanese College Students," *Journal of Social Psychology 145* (2005): 127–140; J. H. Berg, "Responsiveness and Self-Disclosure." In *Self-Disclosure: Theory, Research, and Therapy*, edited by V. Derlega and J. Berg (New York: Plenum, 1987); J. Honeycutt, "A Model of Marital Functioning Based on an Attraction Paradigm and Social-Penetration Dimensions," *Journal of Marriage and the Family 48* (1986): 651–667; G. J. Chelune, E. Waring, B. Yosk, F. Sultan, and J. Ogden, "Self-Disclosure and Its Relationship to Marital Intimacy," *Journal of Clinical Psychology 40* (1984): 216–219; M. Knapp and A. L. Vangelisti, *Interpersonal Communication and Human Relationships* 5e (Boston: Allyn & Bacon, 2005); C. R. Berger and J. J. Bradac, *Language and Social Knowledge: Uncertainty in Interpersonal Relations* (London: Edward Arnold, 1982); S. S. Hendrick, "Self-Disclosure and Marital Satisfaction," *Journal of Personality and Social Psychology 40* (1981): 1150–1159; G. J. Chelune and associates, *Self-Disclosure: Origins, Patterns, and Implications of Openness in Interpersonal Relationships* (San Francisco: Jossey-Bass, 1979); G. R. Miller and M. Steinberg, *Between People: A New Analysis of Interpersonal Communication* (Chicago: Science Research Associates, 1975); G. Levinger and D. Senn, "Disclosure of Feelings in Marriage," *Merrill-Palmer Quarterly 13* (1967): 237–249.

50. D. Borisoff, "The Effect of Gender on Establishing and Maintaining Intimate Relationships." In *Women and Men Communicating: Challenges and Changes* 2e, edited by L. P. Arliss and D. J. Borisoff (Prospect Heights, IL: Waveland, 2001), 15–31; K. Galvin and C. Bylund, "First Marriage Families: Gender and Communication." In Arliss and Borisoff, *Women and Men Communicating*, 132–148; H. T. Reis, "Gender Differences in Intimacy and Related Behaviors: Context and Process." In Canary, *Sex Differences and Similarities in Communication*, 203–231; J. T. Wood and C. C. Inman, "In a Different Mode: Masculine Styles of Communicating Closeness," *Journal of Applied Communication Research 21* (1993): 279–295; K. Dindia and M. Allen, "Sex Differences in Self-Disclosure: A Meta-Analysis," *Psychological Bulletin 112* (1992): 106–124.

51. D. J. Canary and T. M. Emmers-Sommer, with S. Faulkner, *Sex and Gender Differences in Personal Relationships* (New York: Guilford, 1997).

52. E. L. Paul and K. M. White, "The Development of Intimate Relationships in Late Adolescence," *Adolescence 25* (1990): 375–400; J. M. Reisman, "Intimacy in Same-Sex Friendships," *Sex Roles 23* (1990): 65–82; S. Swain, "Covert Intimacy in Men's Friendships: Closeness in Men's Friendships." In *Gender in Intimate Relationships: A Microstructural Approach*, edited by B. Risman and P. Schwartz (Belmont, CA: Wadsworth, 1989), 71–86; R. J. Barth and B. N. Kinder, "A Theoretical Analysis of Sex Differences in Same-Sex Friendships," *Sex Roles 19* (1988): 349–363; B. A. Winstead, "Sex Differences in Same-Sex Friendships." In *Friendship and Social Interaction*, edited by V. J. Derlega and B. A. Winstead (New York: Springer-Verlag, 1986), 81–99.

53. W. K. Rawlins, "Times, Places, and Social Spaces for Cross-Sex Friendship." In Arliss and Borisoff, *Women and Men Communicating*, 93–114.

54. D. Scott, "Marriage Online: Saying 'I Do' by a Virtual Waterfall, Moving into a Virtual House," *Corpus Christi Caller Times* (March 7, 1999): H1, H3.

55. S. Winston, "Cyberlove: Florida Man Gives On-Line Advice for the Lovelorn," *Corpus Christi Caller Times* (May 28, 1995): G1, G7.

56. Wood and Inman, "In a Different Mode."

57. I. Altman and D. Taylor, *Social Penetration: The Development of Relationships* (New York: Holt, Rinehart and Winston, 1973); Brehm. *Intimate Relationships*: B. M. Montgomery, "Communication in Close Relationships." In Weber, *Perspectives on Close Relationships*, 67–87.

58. J. Luft, *Group Process: An Introduction to Group Dynamics* (Palo Alto, CA: Mayfield, 1970).

59. P. Mehta and M. S. Clark, "Toward Understanding Emotions in Intimate Relationships." In Weber, *Perspectives on Close Relationships*, 88–109.

60. A. Hochschild, "The Economy of Gratitude." In *The Sociology of Emotions: Original Essays and Research Papers*, edited by D. Franks and E. D. McCarthy (Greenwich, CT: JAI Press, 1989), 95–113.

61. E. R. McDaniel, "Nonverbal Communication: A Reflection of Cultural Themes." In *Intercultural Communication: A Reader* 8e, edited by L. A. Samovar and R. E. Porter (Belmont, CA: Wadsworth, 1997), 256–265.

62. P. M. Cole, "Children's Spontaneous Control of Facial Expression," *Child Development 57* (1986): 1309–1321.

63. R. W. Simon and L. E. Nath, "Gender and Emotion in the United States: Do Men and Women Differ in Self-Reports of Feelings and Expressive Behavior?" *American Journal of Sociology 109* (2004): 1137–1176; L. K. Guerrero and R. L. Reiter, "Express-

ing Emotion: Sex Differences in Social Skills and Communicative Responses to Anger, Sadness, and Jealousy." In Canary, *Sex Differences and Similarities in Communication*, 321–350; Canary, *Sex and Gender Differences in Personal Relationships*.

64. Jourard, *The Transparent Self*.

65. B. B. Burleson, "Introduction to the Special Issue: Psychological Mediators of Sex Differences in Emotional Support," *Communication Reports 15* (2002): 1–4; W. E. Snell, R. S. Miller, and S. S. Belk, "Development of the Emotional Self-Disclosure Scale," *Sex Roles 18* (1988): 59–73.

66. W. Pollack, *Real Boys: Rescuing Our Sons from the Myths of Boyhood* (New York: Owl Books, 1999); O. Silverstein and B. Rashbaum, *The Courage to Raise Good Men* (New York: Penguin, 1995); V. Monroe, "How to Raise the Men We'd Want to Marry," *O: The Oprah Winfrey Magazine* (June, 2003): 163, 203; P. C. McGraw, "Dr. Phil's MANual," *O: The Oprah Winfrey Magazine* (June, 2003): 46–50; P. C. McGraw, "Dr. Phil: Who *Is* That Masked Man?" *O: The Oprah Winfrey Magazine* (March, 2005): 52, 56.

67. Galvin, "First Marriage Families"; F. Dickson-Markman, "How Important Is Self-Disclosure in Marriage?" *Communication Research Reports 1* (1984): 7–14.

68. A. L. Vangelisti, "Communication Problems in Committed Relationships: An Attributional Analysis." In *Attributions, Accounts, and Close Relationships*, edited by J. H. Harvey, T. L. Orbuch, and A. L. Weber (New York: Springer-Verlag, 1992), 144–164.

69. This chapter benefited from the fine scholarship and work of M. Redmond, coauthor of *Interpersonal Communication: Relating to Others* 4e (Boston: Allyn & Bacon, 2005).

CHAPTER 2.2

1. W. Rawlins, *Friendship Matters: Communication, Dialectics, and the Life Course* (Hawthorne, NY: Aldine de Gruyter, 1992); W. J. Dickens and D. Perlman, "Friendship over the Life-Cycle." In *Personal Relationships 2: Developing Personal Relationships*, edited by S. W. Duck and R. Gilmour (London: Academic Press, 1981).

2. R. Blieszner, "Close Relationships over Time," as reported in J. A. Simpson and B. A. Harris, "Interpersonal Attraction." In *Perspectives on Close Relationships*, edited by A. L. Weber and J. H. Harvey (Boston: Allyn & Bacon, 1994), 1–18.

3. J. Yager, *Friendshifts: The Power of Friendship and How It Shapes Our Lives* (Stamford, CT: Hannacrois Creek Books, 1999); W. Rawlins, "Being There for Friends." In *Making Connections: Readings in Relational Communication*, edited by K. M. Galvin and P. Cooper (Los Angeles: Roxbury, 1996), 258–260; R. Blieszner and

R. Adams, *Adult Friendships* (Newbury Park, CA: Sage, 1992).

4. A. J. Johnson, E. Wittenberg, M. M. Villagran, M. Mazur, and P. Villagran, "Relational Progression as a Dialectic: Examining Turning Points in Communication among Friends," *Communication Monographs 70* (2003): 230–249.

5. P. M. Sias and D. J. Cahill, "From Coworkers to Friends: The Development of Peer Friendships in the Workplace," *Western Journal of Communication 62* (1998): 273–299; G. A. Fine, "Friendships in the Workplace." In Galvin and Cooper, *Making Connections*, 270–277.

6. M. Hughes, K. Morrison, and K. J. K. Asada, "What's Love Got to Do with It? Exploring the Impact of Maintenance Rules, Love Attitudes, and Network Support on Friends with Benefits Relationships," *Western Journal of Communication 69* (2005): 49–66.

7. T. A. Lambert, A. S. Kahn, and K. J. Apple, "Pluralistic Ignorance and Hooking Up," *Journal of Sex Research 40* (2003): 129–133; E. L. Paul and K. A. Hayes, "The Casualties of 'Casual' Sex: A Qualitative Exploration of the Phenomenology of College Students' Hookups," *Journal of Social and Personal Relationships 29* (2002): 639–661; E. L. Paul, B. McManus, and K. A. Hayes, "'Hookups': Characteristics and Correlates of College Students' Spontaneous and Anonymous Sexual Experiences," *Journal of Sex Research 37* (2000): 76–88; W. A. Afifi and S. L. Faulkner, "On Being 'Just Friends': The Frequency and Impact of Sexual Activity in Cross-Sex Friendships," *Journal of Social and Personal Relationships 17* (2000): 205–222.

8. Hughes et al., "What's Love Got to Do With It?"

9. M. Monsour, *Women and Men as Friends: Relationships across the Life Span in the 21st Century* (Mahwah, NJ: Lawrence Erlbaum, 2002).

10. D. Carnegie, *How to Win Friends and Influence People* (New York: Simon & Schuster, 1937).

11. K. Galvin and C. Bylund, "First Marriage Families: Gender and Communication." In *Women and Men Communicating: Challenges and Changes* 2e, edited by L. P. Arliss and D. J. Borisoff (Prospect Heights, IL: Waveland, 2001), 132–148; V. Satir, "The Rules You Live By." In Galvin and Cooper, *Making Connections*, 168–174; S. S. Brehm, R. Miller, D. Perlman, and S. M. Campbell, *Intimate Relationships* 3e (New York: McGraw-Hill, 2001).

12. *The Miami Herald* (July 9, 1982): 12A.

13. M. Coleman, M.A. Fine, L. H. Ganong, K. J. M. Downs, and N. Pauk, "When You're Not the Brady Bunch: Identifying Perceived Conflicts and Resolution Strategies in Stepfamilies," *Personal Relationships 8* (2001): 55–73; D. O. Braithwaite, L. N. Olson, T. D. Golish, C. Soukup, and P. Turman, "'Becoming a Family': Developmental Processes Represented in Blended Family Discourse," *Journal of Applied Communication Research*

29 (2001): 221–247; J. D. Teachman, L. M. Tedrow, and K. D. Crowder, "The Changing Demography of America's Families," *Journal of Marriage and the Family 62* (2000): 1234–1246; J. Hauser, "Communication in the Stepfamily: Transitions Bring Challenges." In Arliss and Borisoff, *Women and Men Communicating*, 149–167; K. M. Galvin and B. J. Brommel, "Communication within Stepfamily Systems." In Galvin and Cooper, *Making Connections*, 239–246.

14. M. M. Kern, "Fighting the Fight." In Galvin and Cooper, *Making Connections*, 247–249.

15. J. Koesten, "Family Communication Patterns, Sex of Subject, and Communication Competence," *Communication Monographs 71* (2004): 226–244.

16. V. Satir, *The New Peoplemaking* (Mountain View, CA: Science & Behavior Books, 1988), 4.

17. *Contexts: A Publication of the American Sociological Association 3* (2004), retrieved from <www.contexts-magazine.org>; AFL-CIO, *National Study of the Changing Workforce* (2002), retrieved from <www.aflcio.org>.

18. National Association of Colleges and Employers, "Job Outlook 2005" (2005) <http://www.jobweb.com>; M. S. Peterson, "Personnel Interviewers' Perceptions of the Importance and Adequacy of Applicants' Communication Skills," *Communication Education 46* (1997): 287–291.

19. H. Mintzberg, "The Manager's Job: Folklore and Fact," *Harvard Business Review 53* (1975): 26–41.

20. J. H. Harvey and A. L. Weber, *Odyssey of the Heart: Close Relationships in the 21st Century* 2e (Mahwah, NJ: Lawrence Erlbaum, 2002); L. K. Guerrero, P. A. Andersen, and W. A. Afifi, *Close Encounters: Communicating in Relationships* (New York: McGraw-Hill 2001); M. L. Knapp and A. Vangelisti, "Relationship Stages: A Communication Perspective." In Galvin and Cooper, *Making Connections*, 134–141; M. L. Knapp and A. L. Vangelisti, *Interpersonal Communication and Human Relationships* 5e (Boston: Allyn & Bacon, 2005); S. A. Welch and R. B. Rubin, "Development of Relationship Stage Measures," *Communication Quarterly 50* (2002): 24–40.

21. A. L. Busboom, D. M. Collins, M. D. Givertz, and L. A. Levin, "Can We Still Be Friends? Resources and Barriers to Friendship Quality after Romantic Relationship Dissolution," *Personal Relationships 9* (2002): 215–223.

22. S. W. Duck, "A Topography of Relationship Disengagement and Dissolution." In *Personal Relationships 4: Dissolving Relationships*, edited by S. W. Duck (New York: Academic Press, 1982); Guerrero, *Close Encounters*.

23. M. L. Knapp, *Social Intercourse: From Greeting to Goodbye* (Boston: Allyn & Bacon, 1978).

24. Duck, "A Topography of Relationship Disengagement and Dissolution."

25. Retrieved February 12, 2004 from <cnn.com>.

26. For research on relationship termination, see S. A. Jang, S. W. Smith, and T. R. Levine, "To Stay or to Leave? The Role of Attachment Styles in Communication Patterns and Potential Termination of Romantic Relationships Following Discovery of Deception," *Communication Monographs 69* (2002): 236–252; S. Metts, "Face and Facework: Implications for the Study of Personal Relationships." In *Handbook of Personal Relationships: Theory, Research, and Interventions*, edited by S. Duck (Chicester, UK: Wiley, 1997), 373–390; B. M. Phillips and J. T. Wood, "The Deterioration Stages in Human Relationships." In Galvin and Cooper, *Making Connections*, 213–218; L. A. Baxter, "Accomplishing Relational Disengagement." In *Understanding Personal Relationships: An Interdisciplinary Approach*, edited by S. Duck and D. Perlman (London: Sage, 1985), 243–265; L. A. Baxter, "Trajectories of Relationship Disengagement," *Journal of Social and Personal Relationships 1* (1984): 29–48; L. A. Baxter, "Strategies for Ending Relationships: Two Studies," *Western Journal of Speech Communication 46* (1982): 223–241; T. L. Morton, J. F. Alexander, and I. Altman, "Communication and Relationships Definition." In *Explorations in Interpersonal Communication*, edited by G. R. Miller (Newbury Park, CA: Sage, 1976), 105–125.

27. L. Stafford, S. L. Kline, and J. Dimmick, "Home E-Mail: Relational Maintenance and Gratification Opportunities," *Journal of Broadcasting & Electronic Media 43* (1999): 659–669.

28. F. S. Christopher and S. Sprecher, "Sexuality in Marriage, Dating, and Other Relationships: A Decade Review." In *Speaking of Sexuality: Interdisciplinary Readings*, edited by J. K. Davidson, Sr., and N. B. Moore (Los Angeles: Roxbury, 2005), 54–71.

29. K. Y. A. McKenna, A. S. Green, and P. K. Smith, "Demarginalizing the Sexual Self," *Journal of Sex Research 38* (2001): 302–316; A. Cooper, I. P. McLoughlin, and K. M. Campbell, "Sexuality in Cyberspace: Update for the 21st Century," *Cyberpsychology & Behavior 3* (2000): 521–536.

30. McKenna et al., "Demarginalizing the Sexual Self."

31. P. C. McGraw, "Couples Combat: The Great American Pastime," *O: The Oprah Winfrey Magazine* (August, 2002): 42–43.

32. M. Deutsch, *The Resolution of Conflict* (New Haven: Yale University Press, 1973).

33. W. W. Wilmot and J. L. Hocker, *Interpersonal Conflict* 6e (New York: McGraw-Hill, 2001).

34. S. Ting-Toomey and L. Chung, *Understanding Intercultural Communication* (Los Angeles: Roxbury, 2003); S. Ting-Toomey and J. G. Oetzel, *Managing Intercultural Conflict Effectively* 2e (Newbury Park, CA: Sage, 2001); S. Ting-Toomey, "Managing Intercultural Conflicts Effectively." In *Intercultural Communication: A*

Reader 8e, edited by L. A. Samovar and R. E. Porter (Belmont, CA: Wadsworth, 1997), 392–404.

35. C. R. Berger, "Social Power and Interpersonal Communication." In *Explorations in Interpersonal Communication.*

36. Brehm, *Intimate Relationships.*

37. P. J. Kalbfleisch and M. J. Cody, eds., *Gender, Power, and Communication in Human Relationships* (Hillsdale, NJ: Lawrence Erlbaum, 1995); L. P. Arliss, "When Myths Endure and Realities Change: Communication in Romantic Relationships." In Arliss and Borisoff, *Women and Men Communicating*, 115–131; F. E. Millar and L. E. Rogers, "Relational Dimensions of Interpersonal Dynamics." In *Interpersonal Process: New Directions in Communication Research*, edited by M. E. Roloff and G. R. Miller (Newbury Park, CA: Sage, 1987), 117–139.

38. D. A. Infante and A. S. Rancer, "Argumentativeness and Verbal Aggressiveness: A Review of Recent Theory and Research," *Communication Yearbook 19* (1996): 319–351; D. A. Infante, B. L. Riddle, C. L. Horvath, and S. A. Tumlin, "Verbal Aggressiveness: Messages and Reasons," *Communication Quarterly 40* (1992): 116–126; D. A. Infante, K. C. Hartley, M. M. Martin, M. A. Higgins, S. D. Bruning, and G. Hur, "Initiating and Reciprocating Verbal Aggression: Effects on Credibility and Credited Valid Arguments," *Communication Studies 43* (1992): 182–190; D. A. Infante, T. C. Sabourin, J. E. Rudd, and E. A. Shannon, "Verbal Aggression in Violent and Nonviolent Marital Disputes," *Communication Quarterly 38* (1990): 361–371; D. A. Infante and C. J. Wigley III, "Verbal Aggressiveness: An Interpersonal Model and Measure," *Communication Monographs 53* (1986): 61–69. For extensions of this line of research on verbal aggression, see K. A. Rocca, "College Student Attendance: Impact of Instructor Immediacy and Verbal Aggression," *Communication Education 53* (2004): 185–195; T. R. Levine, M. J. Beatty, S. Limon, M. A. Hamilton, R. Buck, and R. M. Chory-Assad, "The Dimensionality of the Verbal Aggressiveness Scale," *Communication Monographs 71* (2004): 245–268; R. M. Chory-Assad, "Effects of Television Sitcom Exposure on the Accessibility of Verbally Aggressive Thoughts," *Western Journal of Communication 68* (2004): 431–453; A. D. Heisel, B. H. La France, and M. J. Beatty, "Self-Reported Extraversion, Neuroticism, and Psychoticism as Predictors of Peer Rated Verbal Aggressiveness and Affinity-Seeking Competence," *Communication Monographs 70* (2003): 1–15; G. H. Sherwin and S. Schmidt, "Communication Codes among African American Children and Youth: The Fast Track from Special Education to Prison?" *Journal of Correctional Education 54* (2003): 45–52; P. Schrodt, "Students' Appraisals of Instructors as a Function of Students' Perceptions of Instructors' Aggressive Communication," *Communication Education 52* (2003): 106–121; C. K. Atkin, S. W. Smith, A. J. Roberto, T. Fediuk, and T. Wagner, "Correlates of Verbally Aggressive Communication in Adolescents," *Journal of Applied Communication Research 30* (2002): 251–268; S. A. Myers and K. A. Rocca, "Perceived Instructor Argumentativeness and Verbal Aggressiveness in the College Classroom: Effects on Student Perceptions of Climate, Apprehension, and State Motivation," *Western Journal of Communication 65* (2001): 113–137.

39. Wilmot and Hocker, *Interpersonal Conflict.*

40. C. M. Carey and P. A. Mongeau, "Communication and Violence in Courtship Relationships." In *Family Violence from a Communication Perspective*, edited by D. D. Cahn and S. A. Lloyd (Hillsdale, NJ: Lawrence Erlbaum, 1996), 127–150.

41. P. Yelsma, "Couples' Affective Orientations and Their Verbal Aggressiveness," *Communication Quarterly 43* (1995): 100–114.

42. T. C. Sabourin, "The Role of Negative Reciprocity in Spousal Abuse: A Relational Control Analysis," *Journal of Applied Communication Research 23* (1995): 271–283.

43. Infante et al., "Verbal Aggressiveness."

44. L. N. Olson, "Exploring 'Common Couple Violence' in Heterosexual Romantic Relationships," *Western Journal of Communication 66* (2002): 104–128; T. C. Sabourin and G. H. Stamp, "Communication and the Experience of Dialectical Tensions in Family Life: An Examination of Abusive and Nonabusive Families," *Communication Monographs 62* (1995): 213–242; J. W. White and J. A. Humphrey, "Women's Aggression in Heterosexual Conflicts," *Aggressive Behavior 20* (1994): 195–202.

45. M. M. Martin, C. M. Anderson, and C. L. Horvath, "Feelings about Verbal Aggression: Justifications for Sending, and Hurt from Receiving, Verbally Aggressive Messages," *Communication Research Reports 13* (1996): 19–26; D. Cloven and M. E. Roloff, "The Chilling Effect of Aggressive Potential on the Expression of Complaints in Intimate Relationships," *Communication Monographs 60* (1993): 199–219.

46. Satir, *The New Peoplemaking;* Wilmot and Hocker, *Interpersonal Conflict.*

47. L. L. Putnam and C. E. Wilson, "Communicative Strategies in Organizational Conflicts: Reliability and Validity of a Measurement Scale." In *Communication Yearbook 6*, edited by M. Burgoon (Beverly Hills: Sage, 1982).

48. Cloven and Roloff, "The Chilling Effect of Aggressive Potential on the Expression of Complaints in Intimate Relationships"; Wilmot and Hocker, *Interpersonal Conflict.*

49. M. A. Gross, L. K. Guerrero, and J. K. Alberts, "Perceptions of Conflict Strategies and Communication Competence in Task-Oriented Dyads," *Journal of Applied Communication Research 32* (2004): 249–270.

50. R. Fisher, W. Ury, and B. Patton, *Getting to Yes: Negotiating Agreement without Giving In* 2e (New York: Penguin Books, 1991).

51. This information is based on several excellent discussions of conflict management skills. We acknowledge W. R. Cupach and D. J. Canary, *Competence in Interpersonal Conflict* (Long Grove, IL: Waveland, 2000); D. Borisoff and D. A. Victor, *Conflict Management: A Communication Skills Approach* 2e (Boston: Allyn & Bacon, 1999); D. Yankelovich, *The Magic of Dialogue: Transforming Conflict into Cooperation* (New York: Simon & Schuster, 1999); Wilmot and Hocker, *Interpersonal Conflict*; O. Hargie, ed., *The Handbook of Communication Skills* (London: Routledge, 1997); O. Hargie, C. Saunders, and D. Dickson, *Social Skills in Interpersonal Communication* 3e (London: Routledge, 1994); W. A. Donohue, with R. Holt, *Managing Interpersonal Conflict* (Newbury Park, CA: Sage, 1992); D. A. Romig and L. J. Romig. *Structured Teamwork© Guide* (Austin: Performance Resources, 1990); S. Deep and L. Sussman, *Smart Moves* (Reading, MA: Addison-Wesley, 1990); Fisher, *Getting to Yes*; M. D. Davis, E. L. Eshelman, and M. McKay, *The Relaxation and Stress Reduction Workbook* (Oakland, CA: New Harbinger, 1982); R. Boulton, *People Skills* (New York: Simon & Schuster, 1979).

52. J. B. Rubin, "Stand Back from the Rope!" *O: The Oprah Winfrey Magazine* (March, 2005): 193–194, 197.

53. B. M. Gayle and R. W. Preiss, "Language Intensity Plus: A Methodological Approach to Validate Emotions in Conflicts," *Communication Reports 12* (1999): 43–50; Wilmot and Hocker, *Interpersonal Conflict*.

54. A. Ellis, *A New Guide to Rational Living* (North Hollywood, CA: Wilshire Books, 1977).

55. L. C. Lederman, "The Impact of Gender on the Self and Self-Talk." In Arliss and Borisoff, *Women and Men Communicating*, 78–89; Ellis, *A New Guide to Rational Living*.

56. S. R. Covey, *The Seven Habits of Highly Effective People* (New York: Simon & Schuster, 1989), 67.

57. Fisher, *Getting to Yes*.

APPENDIX A

1. Our discussion of interview questions is based on J. T. Masterson, S. A. Beebe, and N. Watson, *An Invitation to Effective Speech Communication* (Glenview, IL: Scott Foresman and Company, 1989). We especially acknowledge the contributions of Norm Watson to this discussion.

2. This resumé and our suggestions for developing a resumé are based on the 2005 *Texas State University Career Services Manual* (San Marcos, TX: Office of Career Services, 2005).

3. J. L. Winsor, D. B. Curtis, and R. D. Stephens, "National Preferences in Business and Communication Education: A Survey Update," *Journal of the Association for Communication Administration 3* (1997): 174.

4. Adapted from M. S. Hanna and G. Wilson, *Communicating in Business and Professional Settings* (New York: McGraw-Hill, 1991), 263–265.

5. S. Armour, "Employers: Enough Already with the E-Resumés," *USA Today* (July 15, 1999): B1.

6. "Advantages of Web Resumés." April 2, 2005. <http://www.eresumeiq.com/web-resume-advantages.html>.

7. "Advantages of Web Resumés."

8. "Advantages of Web Resumés."

9. "Advantages of Web Resumés."

10. 2005 *Texas State University Career Services Manual*.

APPENDIX B

1. R. D. Gratz and P. J. Salem, "Technology and the Crisis of Self," *Communication Quarterly 32* (1984): 98–103.

2. M. S. Hanna and G. L. Wilson, *Communicating in Business and Professional Settings* 4e (New York: McGraw-Hill, 1998).

3. D. Pescovitz, "Software Robots Simulate Real Conversations," *Corpus Christi Caller Times* (March 21, 1999): D1, D4.

4. Pescovitz, "Software Robots Simulate Real Conversations."

5. L. Strate, "The Varieties of Cyberspace: Problems in Definition and Delimitation," *Western Journal of Communication 63* (1999): 382–412.

6. W. Rousch, "The Internet Reborn." In *Taking Sides: Clashing Views on Controversial Issues in Mass Media and Society* 8e, edited by A. Alexander and J. Hanson (Dubuque, IA: McGraw-Hill/Dushkin, 2005), 224–229; J. J. Jordan, "(Ad)Dressing the Body in Online Shopping Sites," *Critical Studies in Media Communication 20* (2003): 248–268; S. Morreale, "Morreale's Mailbag: 'Blogging' on the Web," *Spectra* (April, 2003): 9.

7. S. Turkle, *Life on the Screen: Identity in the Age of the Internet* (New York: Simon & Schuster, 1995).

8. R. Lee and S. Wahl, "Justifying Surveillance: An Ideological Analysis of the Journalistic Framing of Pedophiles and the Internet." Paper presented at the meeting of the National Communication Association, November, 2003; J. A. McCown, D. Fischer, R. Page, and M. Homant, "Internet Relationships: People Who Meet People," *Cyberpsychology & Behavior 4* (2001): 593–596; J. K. Seale & R. Pockney, "The Use of the Personal Home Page by Adults with Down Syndrome as a Tool for Managing Identity and Friendship,"

British Journal of Learning Disabilities 30 (2002): 142–148.

9. *The Washington Post* (September 29, 2004): A1, as cited in S. Morreale, "Morreale's Mailbag," *Spectra* (November, 2004): 3; J. Wagman, "No LOL Matter: Peer Pressure Pops Up with Instant Messaging," *Corpus Christi Caller Times* (June 22, 2003): A19.

10. M. A. Banks, "Filtering the Net in Libraries." In Alexander and Hanson, *Taking Sides*, 224–229.

11. C. A. Hult and T. N. Huckin, *The New Century Handbook* (Boston: Allyn & Bacon, 1999).

12. T. A. Doyle, *Allyn & Bacon Quick Guide to the Internet for Speech Communication* (Boston: Allyn & Bacon, 1998).

13. K. Y. A. McKenna, A. S. Green, and M. E. J. Gleason, "Relationship Formation on the Internet: What's the Big Attraction?" *Journal of Social Issues 58* (2002): 9–31. For interesting newspaper discussions of cyber-relationships, see "Female Inmates Making Connections—For Good or Ill—On Internet," *Corpus Christi Caller Times* (July 11, 1999): C7; D. Scott, "Marriage Online: Saying 'I Do' By a Virtual Waterfall, Moving into a Virtual House," *Corpus Christi Caller Times* (March 7, 1999): H1, H3; S. Winston, "Cyberlove: Florida Man Gives On-Line Advice for the Lovelorn," *Corpus Christi Caller Times* (May 28, 1995): G1, G7.

14. *New York Times* News Service, "Online Dating No Longer Loser Central," *Corpus Christi Caller Times* (June 29, 2003): A2; Associated Press, "EHarmony Patents Its Formula for Romance," *Corpus Christi Caller Times* (May 30, 2004): A2; R. Konrad, "Dating Site Gets Patent," *Corpus Christi Caller Times* (May 28, 2004): A2; C. Hinojosa, "Couples Say That the Sites Gave Them Time to Learn about Each Other," *Corpus Christi Caller Times* (February 8, 2004): H1, H4.

15. J. Walther and L. Tidwell, "When Is Mediated Communication Not Interpersonal?" In *Making Connections: Readings in Relational Communication*, edited by K. M. Galvin and P. Cooper (Los Angeles: Roxbury, 1996), 300–307.

16. A. Cooper, J. P. McLoughlin, and K. M. Campbell, "Sexuality in Cyberspace: Update for the 21st Century," *Cyberpsychology & Behavior 3* (2000): 521–536.

17. A. N. Markham, *Life Online: Researching Real Experience in Virtual Space* (Walnut Creek, CA: AltaMira Press, 1998), 203.

18. D. Fiely, "Cyber-Infidelity: Internet Access Implicated in Growing Number of Divorces," *The Columbus Dispatch*, Health and Medicine Week [Electronic Version] (2003); "Mental Health: Cybersex Is More Damaging to Relationships Than Pornography," *Cyberpsychology & Behavior 6* (2003): 553; E. R. Merkle and R. A. Richardson, "Digital Dating and Virtual Relating: Conceptualizing Computer-Mediated Romantic Relationships," *Family Relations 9* (2000): 187–196; K. Y. A. McKenna, A. S. Green, and P. K. Smith, "Demarginalizing the Sexual Self," *Journal of Sex Research 38* (2001): 302–316.

19. L. Averyt, "Caught in Adultery's New 'Net,'" *Corpus Christi Caller Times* (September 21, 1997): A1, A10.

20. Hult and Huckin, *The New Century Handbook*; S. McRae, "Coming Apart at the Seams: Sex, Text, and the Virtual Body." In *Wired Women: Gender and New Realities in Cyberspace*, edited by L. Cherny and L. R. Weise (Seattle: Seal Press, 1996), 242–263; L. Kendall, "MUDder? I Hardly Know 'Er! Adventures of a Feminist MUDder." In Cherny and Weise, *Wired Women*, 207–223.

21. H. Rheingold, "The Virtual Community." In Galvin and Cooper, *Making Connections*, 295–299.

22. J. Mahoney, "The E-Mail Explosion: Computer Messaging System Spawns Cultural Revolution," *Austin American-Statesman* (October 11, 1999): A1, A6.

23. Gratz and Salem, "Technology and the Crisis of Self."

24. Averyt, "Caught in Adultery's New 'Net'."

25. D. K. Wysocki, "Let Your Fingers Do the Talking: Sex on an Adult Chatline," *Sexualities 1* (1998): 425–452; Merkle and Richardson, "Digital Dating and Virtual Relating."

26. Walther and Tidwell, "When Is Mediated Communication Not Interpersonal?"

27. J. Barlow, "E-Mail Etiquette Has Its Own Rules," *Houston Chronicle* (March 11, 1999): C1.

Photo Credits

Chapter 2.1: p. 4, © Bob Daemmrich/The Image Works; p. 7, © Spencer Grant/ PhotoEdit; p. 14, © Maya Barnes/The Image Works; p. 21, © Bill Aron/PhotoEdit; p. 27, © Tony Freeman/PhotoEdit.

Chapter 2.2: p. 42, Jack Kurtz/The Image Works; p. 46, © Bob Daemmrich/The Image Works; p. 49, © Jon Riley/Stone/Getty Images; p. 62, © Michael Newman/PhotoEdit.

Appendix A: p. 80, © Bob Daemmrich/The Image Works; p. 98, © Bob Daemmrich/The Image Works.

Appendix B: p. 107, © Reed Saxon/AP/Wide World Photos.

Answers to Practice Tests

CHAPTER 2.1

Multiple Choice

1. d	11. a
2. d	12. c
3. c	13. b
4. c	14. c
5. c	15. c
6. a	16. a
7. c	17. a
8. d	18. d
9. d	19. c
10. a	20. a

True/False

1. T
2. T
3. F
4. T
5. F
6. F
7. T
8. T
9. F
10. F

Fill in the Blank

1. interactive
2. choice
3. interpersonal
4. self-disclosure
5. circumstance
6. attraction
7. uncertainty-reduction
8. passive
9. impersonal
10. matching

CHAPTER 2.2

Multiple Choice

1. a	11. b
2. c	12. d
3. c	13. a
4. a	14. d
5. b	15. a
6. b	16. d
7. c	17. c
8. c	18. c
9. c	19. d
10. a	20. c

True/False

1. T
2. F
3. F
4. T
5. F
6. T
7. F
8. F
9. F
10. T

Fill in the Blank

1. constructive
2. escalation
3. conflict
4. destructive
5. power
6. cooperative
7. aggressive
8. nonconfrontational
9. confrontational
10. de-escalation

Key to the MyCommunicationLab Media Assets

The MyCommunicationLab assets are listed by type and title in the order in which they appear throughout each chapter.

CHAPTER 2.1

Explore	Interpersonal Communication: Self-Disclosure
Watch	Juggling Act
Quick Review	What Is Interpersonal Communication?
Homework	Metacommunication Challenge
Watch	Time Troubles
Watch	Do You Come Here Often?
Watch	Power Moment
Quick Review	Initiating Relationships
Watch	Self-Disclosure: Friends
Visual Literacy	Self-Disclosure and Relational Development: A Long and Intimate Relationship
Watch	Aisha's Paper
Profile	Johari Window
Visual Literacy	The Johari Window Model Pane Size Varies with Different Amounts of Self-Disclosure
Watch	The Saga of Susan and Juan
Watch	Swim Team
Quick Review	Maintaining Relationships

CHAPTER 2.2

Watch	The Name Game
Quick Review	The Importance of Friendship
Watch	Fast Food
Quick Review	The Importance of Family
Watch	Trust Troubles
Watch	What Was That?
Quick Review	The Importance of Colleagues
Visual Literacy	Self-Disclosure and Relational Development
Watch	The Saga of Susan and Juan
Visual Literacy	Intra-psychic Phase
Visual Literacy	Grave Dressing Phase
Visual Literacy	Dyadic Phase
Explore	Relationships
Visual Literacy	Social Phase
Quick Review	Stages of Relationship Development
Homework	Letting It Go
Watch	Power Moment
Watch	Drive Me Nuts
Watch	Going Up
Watch	Art Appreciation
Watch	Time Troubles
Watch	The Team Project
Profile	Dealing with Conflict
Watch	Job Promotion

Watch	Aisha's Paper
Watch	Helping Annie
Watch	The Reunion
Quick Review	Managing Interpersonal Conflict

APPENDIX A

Explore	Interviewing

Index

Notes

Notes

Notes

Notes